The Pennine Way

by Tom Stephenson

Long Distance Footpath Guide No 1

London Her Majesty's Stationery Office 1969

Published for the Countryside Commission

Inside front cover:
The road over Long Man Hill
Pages vi and vii:
View from Cairn Hill, on the Cheviots,
looking towards the Simonside Hills,
near Rothbury
Inside back cover:
Gordale Scar, Malham

The maps in this guide are extracts from
Ordnance Survey 1 Inch and 1:25,000
(approximately 2½ Inches to 1 Mile) maps.
They have been prepared from production
material supplied by Ordnance Survey.
1 Inch: Sheet Nos. 70, 71, 76, 77, 83, 84,
90, 95, 101 and 102. 1:25,000: Sheet Nos.
NY63, NY73, SE00, SK08, SK09 and
SK18.

Drawings by Harry Titcombe

© Crown copyright 1969
First published 1969
Third impression 1973

Government Bookshops
49 High Holborn, London WC1V 6HB
13a Castle Street, Edinburgh EH2 3AR
109 St Mary Street, Cardiff CF1 1JW
Brazennose Street, Manchester M60 8AS
50 Fairfax Street, Bristol BS1 3DE
258 Broad Street, Birmingham B1 2HE
80 Chichester Street, Belfast BT1 4JY

*Government publications are also available
through booksellers*

**Prepared for the Countryside
Commission by the Central
Office of Information**

Printed in England for Her Majesty's Stationery office
by Hindson Print Group Ltd, Newcastle upon Tyne
SBN 11   700480 4 Dd 503663 K 80

Maps

Difficult Routes

This waymark symbol is
used in plaque or stencil
form by the Countryside
Commission on long-
distance footpaths and
bridleways

Preface

The Pennine Way, the longest footpath in Britain, runs from the Peak District to the Scottish Border. As the first Long Distance Footpath to be completed it is already well established in the public eye. In 1965, its first year, a survey on four days in the summer holiday period showed that half of those passing some 15 checkpoints were on walks lasting more than 10 days, and that nearly a third intended to walk the whole 250 miles. Clearly the Way is providing a challenge that many find exciting. It does so in an age which leaves us fewer and fewer opportunities to use our legs for walking, and our eyes and ears for sights and sounds that have not changed over centuries.

The Way crosses some of the roughest and most remote country in England, but other parts lie within

easy reach of densely populated areas. Almost
anywhere on its length the high moors can still
provide quietness and solitude for those whose
day-to-day life is too noisy, too dirty or
too crowded.

It gives me particular pleasure to introduce
Mr. Stephenson's book since he originated the idea
of the Pennine Way and can really claim to have
laid its foundations. It has, however, taken
30 years of patient negotiation before the whole
length of the Way could be opened. At the rate
of $8\frac{1}{3}$ miles a year these Long Distance Footpaths
are like oaks in comparison with the mushroom
growth of motorways, but I am sure that they will be as
enduring as oaks and a no less valuable
enrichment of our national scene.

Wootton of Abinger

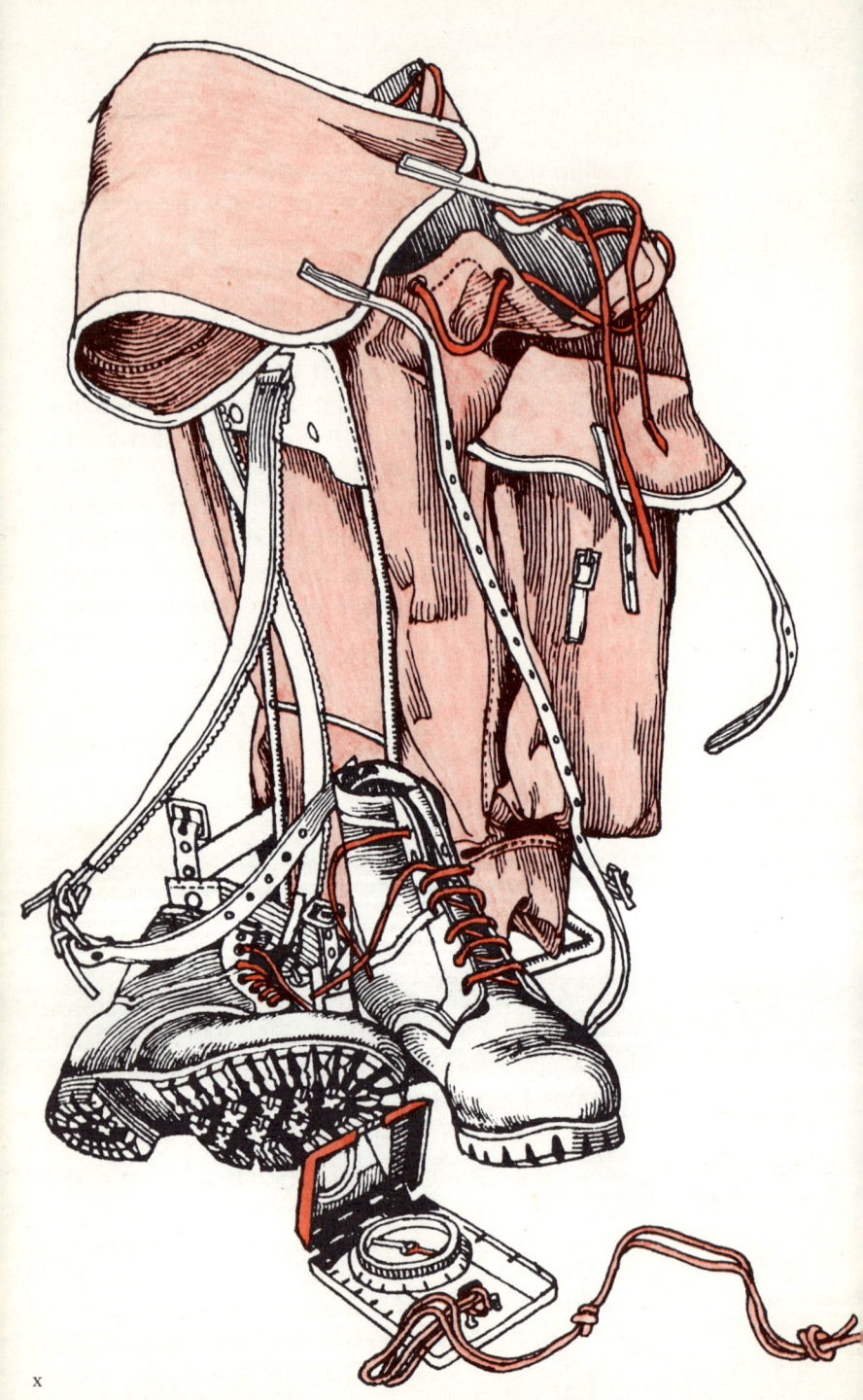

CHAPTER ONE

The Beginnings

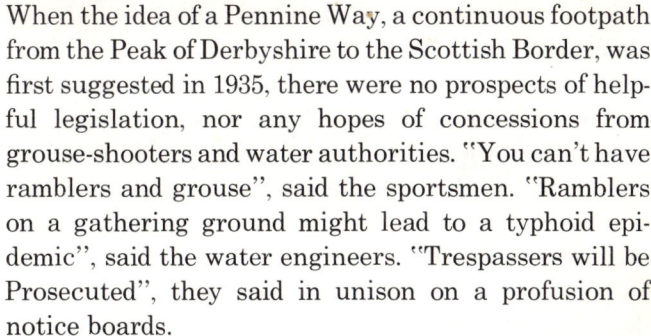

When the idea of a Pennine Way, a continuous footpath from the Peak of Derbyshire to the Scottish Border, was first suggested in 1935, there were no prospects of helpful legislation, nor any hopes of concessions from grouse-shooters and water authorities. "You can't have ramblers and grouse", said the sportsmen. "Ramblers on a gathering ground might lead to a typhoid epidemic", said the water engineers. "Trespassers will be Prosecuted", they said in unison on a profusion of notice boards.

For fifty years, Parliament had repeatedly thrown out an Access to Mountains Bill which proposed that, subject to certain provisions, no owner or occupier of uncultivated mountain or moorland should be entitled to exclude any person from walking or being on such land for the purpose of recreation or for scientific or artistic study.

A Bill introduced by Mr. A. Creech Jones in December 1938 did reach the Statute Book as the Access to Mountains Act 1939, but it suffered from being a Private Member's Bill which could not provide for compensation, and it was so amended in Committee as to be unacceptable to ramblers, who had long campaigned for "freedom of the hills". This Act was never applied and was repealed by the National Parks and Access to the Countryside Act 1949.

After the first world war, increasing numbers of townspeople turned to the countryside for recreation. Rambling clubs and federations of clubs increased in numbers. In 1930 the Youth Hostels Association (England and Wales) was founded, and the opening of 1 hostels providing meals and accommodation at low charges made it possible for young people of limited means to spend weekends and holidays in the country. Over most of England and Wales they were able to do so without restriction, but in some parts of the Pennines, and particularly at the southern end, things were different. Kinder Scout, a dozen square miles of moorland at the start of the Pennine Way, was uncrossed by any right of way. Bleaklow (37 square miles), farther north, was similarly devoid of footpaths. These and adjacent moors were strictly preserved for grouse-shooting.

There was a good deal of trespassing and occasional clashes between ramblers and gamekeepers. Thousands of ramblers from Manchester and Sheffield attended annual access-to-mountains demonstrations in the Winnats, near Castleton. In 1932 some four hundred people met at Hayfield for a widely advertised "mass trespass" on Kinder Scout. The inevitable happened; some of the demonstrators were involved in scuffles with police and gamekeepers, and five of the ringleaders were later sentenced to terms of imprisonment.

So my suggestion in a newspaper article of June 1935 of a Pennine Way had a timely, though unpremeditated, appeal. Instead of being forgotten within a few days, it led to an insistent, popular demand for the creation of such a path, and in February 1938 representatives of open-air organisations met at Hope, Derbyshire, and formed the Pennine Way Association.

The conference called for immediate steps to be taken to create the Way, it being agreed that:

"The wide, health-giving moorlands and high places of solitude, the features of natural beauty and the places of historical interest along the Pennine Way give this route a special character and attractiveness which should be available for all time as a natural heritage of the youth of the country and of all who feel the call of the hills and the lonely places."

Local committees then surveyed the route, which had been planned to use, as far as possible, existing paths, including grass-grown Roman roads and tracks once used by miners, shepherds and drovers. By the end of 1939 it had been established that there were about 180 miles of presumed rights of way and that 70 miles of new paths were required.

In 1942, the Committee on Land Utilisation in Rural Areas recommended the provision of national and regional parks; the setting up of a Footpaths Commission; the recognition of such "hikers' highways" as the Pennine Way; and the re-opening of the old coastguard path round the coast of England and Wales. Next, in 1945, came the Dower Report on National Parks in England and Wales, which included recommendations that the Pennine Way and other long-distance routes should be put into execution as soon as possible.

The Hobhouse Committee reported in 1947 on National Parks, as did the Special Committee on Footpaths and Access to the Countryside (also under the chairmanship of Sir Arthur Hobhouse). The latter committee recommended the creation of the following long-distance routes: Pennine Way; Chilterns to Devon Coast; Pilgrims Way; South Downs to Salisbury Plain; Offa's Dyke; and the Thames Towpath.

The National Parks and Access to the Countryside Act 1949 provided for the establishment of a National Parks Commission which, among other duties, was charged with the responsibility of submitting to the Minister proposals for the creation of long-distance routes.

The Commission decided to start with the Pennine Way and adopted, with minor variations, the route surveyed by ramblers in 1939.

In their second annual report the Commission said:

"The Pennine Way will be a strenuous high-level route through predominantly wild country and is intended for walkers of some experience. It will involve a fair element of physical exertion and a willingness to endure rough going. While the greater part of the Way is across existing well-trodden tracks, the route in places crosses expanses of wild moorland devoid of prominent landmarks and consisting largely of peat, heather, bog and tussocks of rough grass. These sections of the route can be traversed only by strong walkers, and in bad weather they can be safely negotiated only by people who can steer a course by map and compass."

On 6th July, 1951, Mr. Hugh Dalton, then Minister of Local Government and Planning, approved the route put forward by the Commission, and it then remained for the local authorities to negotiate for the creation of the new rights of way required. On 24th April, 1965, Lord Strang, then chairman of the National Parks Commission, Mr. F. T. Willey, then Minister of Land and Natural Resources, and the author, as Secretary of the Ramblers' Association, addressed an audience of more than 2,000 gathered on Malham Moor to celebrate the completion of the Pennine Way.

Bilberry (*Vaccinium myrtillus*)

CHAPTER TWO

The Pennines

Pennine Chain, backbone of England, is a cliché the geographers will no longer tolerate. The Pennines, they say, are not a chain, not a range, only a "broad uplift". Even the name is illegitimate, with no better ancestry than a literary forgery. Charles Bertram, a young professor of English in Copenhagen, claimed in 1747 to have discovered a fourteenth-century monkish chronicle, *De Statu Britanniae,* which described the state of Britain in Roman times. Britannia Maxima, the manuscript said, was divided into two equal parts by a chain of mountains called the Penine Alps *(Alpes Penina).* This led two early geologists, Conybeare and Phillips, writing in 1822, to adopt the name "Penine", which later gained an additional "n". Although the manuscript was proved to be an invention of Bertram's, many of his fictitious names of Roman sites found their way onto Ordnance Survey maps, and some have lingered in maps and guide-books until recent years. Thus, the Roman camps at Chew Green in the Cheviots are still named on some maps as Ad Fines.

Bertram may have been inspired by a passage in Camden's *Britannia* which first appeared in a Latin edition in 1586 and subsequently in various English editions. The following quotation is from Bishop Edmund Gibson's translation published in 1695 and again in 1722: "The north part of the county (Staffordshire) rises gently into small hills; which begin here, and, like the Apennine in Italy, run through the middle of England in one continued ridge, rising higher and higher, as far as Scotland, under several names: for here they are called Moorland, after that the Peak, then

Blackstone Edge, anon Craven, next Stanmore, and last of all, when they branch out into horns, Cheviot."

Except for some inliers of older rocks, the Pennines consist of Carboniferous strata and can, for our purpose, be regarded as made up of three main divisions. First is the Carboniferous Limestone which, though well exposed at Castleton, just south of Edale, is not seen as we go northwards until we are near Skipton. Above the limestone are the Yoredale rocks consisting

Geology of the Greater Pennine region

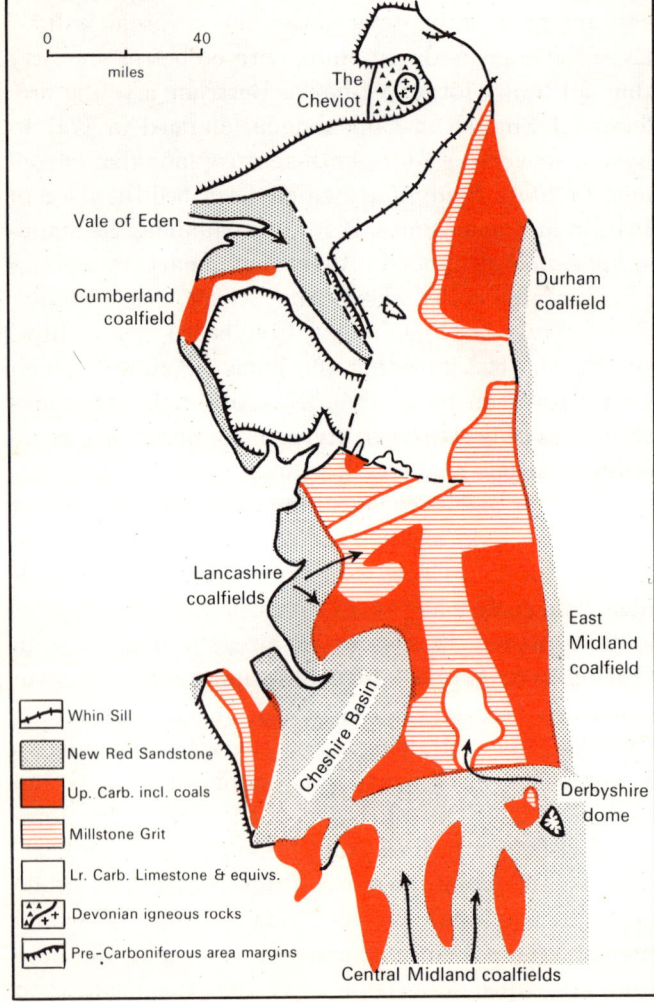

of beds of less pure limestone, shales and sandstones. Overlying these and capping the hilltops is the Millstone Grit.

In Ribblesdale, the limestone may be seen resting on upturned beds of Ordovician and Silurian rocks, the roots of mountains which had been worn down before subsiding beneath the sea of Carboniferous times. Before that took place, during the Devonian period, great thicknesses of Old Red Sandstone accumulated

Vertical section, Fountains Fell to Malham

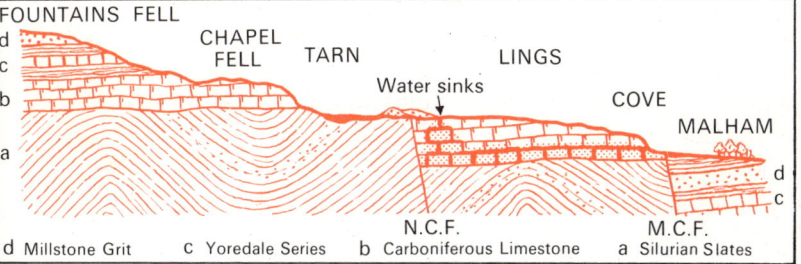

d Millstone Grit   c Yoredale Series   b Carboniferous Limestone   a Silurian Slates

N.C.F. North Craven Fault   M.C.F. Mid-Craven Fault

in Scotland and in the Welsh Border counties, while in Northumberland, where Cheviot now stands, there was a large volcano pouring out ashes and lava into which the granite of Cheviot itself was later intruded.

Corals and other creatures flourished in the clear waters of the early Carboniferous sea. The accumulation of their shells and skeletons and the deposition of calcareous detritus over a vast length of time built up great masses of limestone.

Gradually the delta of a northern river extended southwards carrying mud and sand into areas where limestone had been accumulating. During this time the sea floor was slowly sinking at an irregular rate. Sometimes the deposition of a river-borne material was sufficient to create shallow-water conditions and form sand-flats. When the rate of subsidence was quicker, only fine mud reached the sea, the coarser materials being deposited farther north. At other times even the mud was not brought so far south and limestone would again accumulate. In this way the alternating beds of limestone, shale and sandstone were formed. These are the Yoredale rocks, so named because they were first studied in Wensleydale, the old name of which was Yoredale.

In the next phase, rivers flowing from a continent including Greenland, Scotland and Scandinavia, spread deposits of sand and mud over an extensive delta to form the Millstone Grit, some beds of which were once quarried for millstones, hence the name. Professor Kendall calculated that the Millstone Grit originally extended over more than 25,000 square miles. Assuming an average thickness of half a mile, he estimated the amount of sediment involved would require the destruction of "a mountain range 600 miles long, 20 miles broad at the base, and two miles high".

From Kinder Scout to Cross Fell these grits form the "Edges" (Standedge, Blackstone Edge) and cap the hills, sometimes with level tops, as on Ingleborough, Great Shunner Fell and Cross Fell.

The delta in which these deposits accumulated became shallower and formed estuarine swamps in which

Geological sections through Cross Fell and Murton Fell (much simplified)

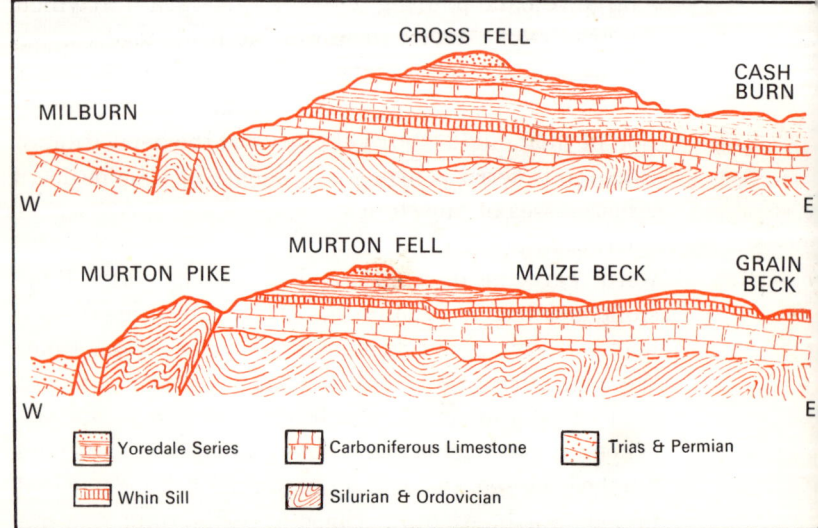

tree-like plants flourished and their remains piled up to produce the coal measures. This stage marked the close of the Carboniferous, and was followed by a period of earth movement and uplifting of the strata. South of Skipton the rocks were raised to form a gentle arch or anticline. Northwards from there the strata have a slight inclination to the east with a series of great faults or fractures, making steep scarps along the western margin.

Towards the close of Carboniferous times a sheet of dolerite was intruded in the strata over a wide area from the Farne Isles to Cross Fell and Upper Teesdale. This is the Whin Sill, which is responsible for the waterfalls of High Force and Caldron Snout, the columnar crags fringing High Cup Nick and the heights, followed by Hadrian's Wall from the Nine Nicks of Thirlwall to Sewingshields.

In the Eden Valley, Permian and Triassic strata abut against Carboniferous rocks. These beds, which together constitute the New Red Sandstone, accumulated in desert conditions during a long period of denudation after the mountain-building period. Except for surface deposits of the Ice Age, they are the youngest strata we shall encounter on the Pennine Way. Any rocks deposited subsequently have been worn away, as have the Coal Measures, which once covered the whole area, but are now found only in the coalfields on each side of the Pennines.

In Tertiary times there was another period of mountain building which piled up the Alps, the Andes and the Himalayas and also gave the land with which we are here concerned a further uplift. From this newly raised ridge rivers began to carve their valleys. Then, in geologically recent times, came the Ice Age, when all except the highest parts of the Pennines were buried beneath an ice sheet. Glaciers smoothed the hillsides, broadened and scoured the valleys, and as they retreated, plastered the lower ground with moraines and layers of clay and boulders.

The Pennines are, in fact, the remains of a plateau in which rivers have carved their valleys. They fall into 9 three distinct areas: the moorlands from Derbyshire to the Aire Gap; a central group from the Aire to Stainmore, and the High Pennines between Stainmore and Tynedale. At the southern end, Kinder Scout and Bleaklow are just over 2,000 feet, but there is a decrease in the general height down to about 1,300 feet near Skipton. North of the Aire Gap the moors are higher, and often exceed 2,000 feet.

Although many of the heights are specifically named as Kinder Scout, Great Shunner Fell and Cross Fell, they seldom have any separate identity beyond perhaps a slight rise above the general level of the surrounding moorland. Ingleborough and Pen-y-ghent, from some aspects, appear to stand alone as individual peaks, but even they have long shoulders.

There is none of the ruggedness of Tryfan or Scafell; no splintered peaks like the Cuillin of Skye. Instead, here are great stretches of shaggy moorland; long ridges dipping sharply to the valleys and gently swelling heights repeating themselves with minor variations into the blue distance; vast solitudes with no sounds other than of running water, or of the wind swishing in the heather or rustling in the grass.

In August the heather moors flaunt their royal purple, but even in mid-winter, when blooms and leaves have withered, they still add a dominant and not unpleasing though sombre note. Then they appear as large expanses of sooty black perhaps fringed with silver-grey grass. The moor grass is often bleached to a pale grey, there is a red tinge on the cotton-grass; the rushes are copper-hued and the bracken a riot of colour. At other times pastel tints predominate, brushed in great sweeps; the soft greens of heather and bilberry, the emerald of sphagnum and the blue-green of the moor grass.

The Pennines are not, in fact, as black as they are painted, although they have their sombre reaches. Places which, to eyes accustomed to softer, downland country, may appear the abomination of desolation, have a fascination for many northern ramblers and others who have acquired a taste for such scenes.

Thomas Hardy said of Egdon Heath that it "appealed

to a subtler and scarcer instinct, to a more recently learned emotion, than that which responds to a sort of beauty called charming and fair". Compared with the summits of Bleaklow or Black Hill or the wastes around Tees Head, "Haggard Egdon" would indeed seem almost fair. On these and other heights there are large expanses of black peat, sometimes intersected with numerous channels locally known as groughs, and maybe with a central bog or moss.

Where the word moss appears on the map one may expect to find a boggy place with spongy, green carpets of sphagnum, with here and there crimson tufts of *Sphagnum rubellum,* or an expanse of cotton-grass *(Eriophorum)* growing in clumps, and in summer flecked with its snow-white fruits. In these mosses too may be found bog myrtle *(Myrica gale),* bog asphodel *(Narthecium ossifragum),* the two insectivorous plants, sundew *(Drosera rotundifolia)* and butterwort *(Pinguicula vulgaris),* cloud berry *(Rubus chamaemorus),* crowberry *(Empetrum nigrum)* and, more rarely, bog rosemary *(Andromeda polifolia).* Above the mosses there is, in some places, higher ground which is better drained and may be clothed with ling *(Calluna vulgaris)* or bilberry *(Vaccinium myrtillus).* Fringing the mosses, and rippling in the wind, there may be expanses of purple moor grass *(Molinia).*

Other large areas are covered with ling or heather. In fact, to most people, heather and moor are almost synonymous. Associated with the predominant ling there may be bell-heather *(Erica cinerea)* and cross-leaved heather *(Erica tetralix),* yellow tormentil *(Potentilla erecta),* and creeping bedstraw *(Galium saxatile).*

It has long been a practice to burn the heather periodically to get rid of the old growth and make way for young more succulent shoots, and so to provide better feed for grouse or sheep, or both. Where the moor has been burnt too frequently or over-grazed, the heather may have been replaced by grey mat grass *(Nardus stricta).* This, like the cotton-grass and the purple moor grass, forms tussocks known on the Border as Scotsmen's heads.

Round the moor edges bilberry is usually found, and in August, on ledges where the sheep have not cropped the plants, the luscious, purple berries may be gathered.

On some moors, streams and rivulets have carved numerous channels in the peat, some of them ten or twelve feet deep. The intersection of the streams, aided by wind erosion, has then produced isolated mushroom-shaped hummocks capped with heather or bilberry.

On the hillsides the mat grass may still appear, but bent *(Agrostis)* and sheep's fescue *(Festuca ovina)* are usually dominant. These grassy slopes, however, may have been invaded by the spread of bracken which, though it may delight the eye with its vernal green or its autumnal russet, gold and bronze, is of little use to the farmer.

If the moorland heights generally have a limited flora, this is more than compensated for by the profusion and variety to be found on the lower slopes and in the dales. The limestone districts of Craven in Yorkshire, and Upper Teesdale (the Yorkshire side of which was declared a National Nature Reserve in September 1963) have long been famous among botanists.

Here we can mention only a few species. In moist places the handsome yellow globe flower *(Trollius europaeus)* and the Grass of Parnassus *(Parnassia palustris),* as lovely as its name, may be seen.

On the scree at Malham Cove grows Jacob's ladder or Greek valerian *(Polemonium caeruleum)*; there the botanist John Ray discovered it about 280 years ago.

In the crevices or "grikes" in the limestone flourish beautiful ferns such as harts-tongue *(Phyllitis scolopendrium),* common polypody *(Polypodium vulgare)* and green spleenwort *(Asplenium viride)*. Other flowers of the limestone are alpine penny cress *(Thlaspi alpestre),* alpine cinquefoil *(Potentilla crantzii),* small meadow rue *(Thalictrum minus),* common rockrose *(Helianthemum chamaecistus)* and the mountain pansy *(Viola lutea).*

Harry Titcombe

13

On Malham Moor and in Upper Teesdale, the bird's-eye primrose *(Primula farinosa)* is to be found.

Spring sandwort *(Arenaria verna)* grows in a number of places, and the Yorkshire sandwort *(Arenaria gothica),* is not known to occur anywhere else in the United Kingdom. Ingleborough and Pen-y-ghent are noted as habitats of the purple saxifrage *(Saxifraga oppositifolia).*

The flora of Teesdale, it has been said, is perhaps better known than that of any other mountainous area in Britain. Here flourishes the spring gentian *(Gentiana verna),* the Teesdale violet *(Viola rupestris),* the bog sandwort *(Minuartia stricta),* and three species of lady's mantle *(Alchemilla).*

Among other plants found here are the shrubby cinquefoil *(Potentilla fruticosa),* mountain avens *(Dryas octopetala),* alpine bartsia *(Bartsia alpina),* and alpine forget-me-not *(Myosotis alpestris),* and several species of orchis.

While we have mentioned some of the rare species, we have done so confident that walkers on the Pennine Way will be content to admire them on the ground and to leave them for others to enjoy. We are confident also that walkers will realise the importance of observing at all times the other maxims of the Country Code set out in pages 107-109. Strict adherence to these rules is of prime importance to the conservation of the country-side, its life and its work.

Bird life is plentiful in the valleys, and in addition to the commoner species, we may see or hear various warblers, pied, yellow and grey wagtails.

Along a stream side a kingfisher may flash by, a dipper may bob from stone to stone, or a sandpiper dart past with its frantic cry. The nesting places of great crested and little grebes are known to naturalists. Buzzards, ravens and the peregrine falcon nest in some of the crags—the last-mentioned species accounts for the name of the Falcon Clints in Upper Teesdale.

The lapwing or green plover, particularly in the breeding season, will wheel and wail with maddening persistence round and ahead of any intruder. On the moors grouse will rise with a startling flutter of wings and a raucous cry of "go-back-back-back". Far more pleasing is the haunting, bubbling cry of the curlew. Northumberland National Park Committee have chosen a drawing of the curlew as their emblem; but for that it might well have been the symbol of the Pennine Way.

Butterwort (*Pinguicula vulgaris*)

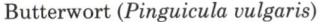

CHAPTER THREE

Edale to Malham

From Edale, at its southern end, the Pennine Way makes a deceptively easy start. After crossing the Grinds Brook between banks of black, crumbling shale, a well-trodden path mounts steadily up the valley towards the rock-rimmed Edale Moor—an eastern shoulder of Kinder Scout.

Half an hour of easy walking leads to the foot of a side-stream alongside which there is a steep ascent to the moor edge. Here the gritstone has weathered into weird and fantastic forms, some of which might have been shaped by Henry Moore.

From this point the Way runs westwards along one of several peat channels or "groughs", and then crosses other groughs draining from north to south. It then continues, still westwards, towards a group of weathered blocks of gritstone and beyond them to Crowden Brook. Downstream are the rocks of Crowden Tower, and farther west another group of stones known as the Wool Packs. One of these, recognisable by its two horns, is named Pym Chair.

To the north-west, a cairn marks the highest point of Kinder (2,088 ft.)—a scarcely perceptible rise above the general level. To the north, Crowden Head (2,070 ft.) is similarly inconspicuous. Ahead, the ground is intersected with innumerable peat channels, but the northward-leading grough of Crowden Brook takes one into the boggy centre of Kinder where, except after a prolonged drought, progress can be made only with some floundering from one less boggy patch to another.

After about 300 yards of this bog-hopping, and keeping west of the now discernible slight rise of Crowden Head, one should slither down a steep bank of peat to the head-stream of Kinder River.

Mrs. Humphry Ward, in *The History of David Grieve,* perhaps only exaggerated slightly when she said of this summit that it was "a vast black glacier, whereof the crevasses are great fissures, ebon black in colour, sometimes ten feet deep".

Withins

The Kinder River is now followed downstream, with tracks first on one side and then the other, or occasionally along the river bed, and so to Kinder Gates, where the stream has worn a way through a band of gritstone. Onwards the stream leads to Kinder Downfall where it plunges a hundred feet or so over the rocky lip of the moor, except when a good south-westerly breeze flings the water upwards in a cloud of spray.

All ways over Kinder seem to lead to the Downfall,[1] and on any weekend, in fair weather or foul, ramblers congregate here—and so do the sheep, hungrily waiting for unwanted scraps of food.

Beyond the Downfall the going, for a short while, is easier and drier down a north-westerly shoulder to Mill Hill. There the Way crosses a famous path running from Hayfield up William Clough to the watershed and down Ashop Clough to the Snake Inn. The Peak District and Northern Counties Footpaths Preservation Society, founded in 1894, appealed for £1,000 to cover the costs

[1] See page 90 for the alternative and easier route from Edale to the Downfall.

Leeds and Liverpool Canal, near Skipton

of litigation to establish their claim that this was an ancient right of way. The landowners concerned, however, after prolonged negotiation, agreed to the dedication of a right of way. On 29th May, 1897, the path was opened by members of the Society walking from the Snake Inn to Hayfield, where they were welcomed by the village brass band.

By Moss Castle and Featherbed Top (significant names) the Way runs to the Snake road and beyond it crosses Doctor's Gate, a Roman road, and then follows the Devil's Dike, a trench running in a straight line for half a mile to a group of four stakes on Alport Low. Between this point and Bleaklow Head (2,061 ft.) there are more groughs to be negotiated, for Bleaklow is much like Kinder Scout but there is more of it. Except for isolated hummocks, the peat has been stripped from the summit, leaving a sandy soil speckled with quartz pebbles. Five miles away, as the crow flies, and almost due north is the soaring BBC television mast on Holme Moss. A bearing four or five degrees west of the mast leads to Wildboar Grain, which is easily followed to a 19 confluence at John Track Well.[2] A strip of green sphagnum marks this oasis where, in a small rock cavity, there is clear sparkling water instead of the peat-stained brew of the streams.

From this point the stream is left for a track by Clough Edge, down to Longdendale. Two hundred yards west of the track is Torside Castle, a pear-shaped, prehistoric mound, distinguished by the lighter tint of its covering vegetation. This mound may account for the name Bleaklow; low being derived from the Old English *hlaew,* meaning a burial mound or, secondarily, a hill.

Out of Longdendale, the valley of the River Etherow, now occupied by a chain of reservoirs belonging to Manchester Corporation, there is a climb of some eleven hundred feet to the summit of Black Hill or Soldier's Lump (1,908 ft.).

From here, for those desiring a change from bog-hopping, there is an escape route (see page 91) down Hey Clough and then to the road A635 and down the Wessenden Valley, and then over the moors to Standedge. The shorter high-level route runs north-westerly to A635 and then crosses White Moss and Black Moss on the way to Standedge. Here the Pennines have narrowed considerably—a fact which led to the making of the canal and railway tunnels under, and the road over, Standedge, linking Lancashire and Yorkshire.

Beyond the road A62, the Way follows the escarpment by Millstone Edge and the Dinner Stone to Northern Rotcher. On this edge a bronze plaque commemorates Ammon Wrigley, a locally born dialect poet and author, whose ashes were scattered here in 1948.

Down below to the west is "the frayed Pennine edge of urban Lancashire", but northwards and eastwards there is still wave beyond wave of moorland, of heather and bilberry and cotton-grass.

20   A cairned route leads to the road A640. Just as it reaches the road the Way joins an old packhorse track. Three hundred yards back along the track a stone lying

[2] See page 90 for additional notes.

on the ground is inscribed "P.H. Road", reminder of a legal contest in 1908—a leading case now quoted in the law books on rights of way. Marsden Urban District Council had repaired an ancient packhorse road, and marked the route across the moor with guide posts. The lord of the manor maintained that the track was not a right of way and called for removal of the posts. When the case was heard numerous witnesses testified to having used the track. Mrs. Hannah Bolton said that her mother, born in 1788, used to say, "when it was fine you could hear the bell horses coming down from the tops". Sam Garside, an eighty-year-old shepherd, remembered, when twelve years old, returning from Marsden Fair at eleven o'clock at night leading a "tup" by a rope and steering a drunken father. The judge ruled that the track was a right of way, but the public must take the track as they found it, and the erection of the guide posts was a trespass.

22   Beyond the road A672 and after passing the wireless station on Windy Hill, the Pennine Way crosses the Trans-Pennine Motorway M62 and then follows the Lancashire-West Riding boundary on to Blackstone Edge. Here on the gritstone crags with massive blocks tumbled at their feet is Robin Hood's Bed.

At a solitary standing stone (Aiggin Stone[3]) the Way crosses the line of a Roman road: a paved way with grooved stones down the centre, about the origin of which antiquarians are still arguing.

Blackstone Edge, said Celia Fiennes, was "noted all over England for a dismal high precipice and steep in the ascent and descent on Either End".

Daniel Defoe, in August 1724, when the ground was so covered with snow that no track was visible, also found "a fearful precipice". Over what he termed "the Andes of England", there is now a regular bus service, and a constant flow of lorries between the Lancashire and Yorkshire towns.

Five miles north of Blackstone Edge, and visible from its highest point, is Stoodley Pike, with a tower 120 feet

[3] This stone has been toppled over in recent years.

high, originally built to commemorate the peace following the Battle of Waterloo, and twice rebuilt. Below the Pike is the Calder Valley; so narrow that road, river, railway and canal fill the valley floor between Todmorden and Hebden Bridge.

Beyond the valley the Way climbs only to drop again to the Colden Water, and then up and over Heptonstall Moor to the upper reaches of Hebden Water, some five miles upstream from Hardcastle Crags, where fifty years ago Lancashire and Yorkshire people used to come in wagonettes for a day's outing.

Drystone walls are a common feature of the Pennines, but nowhere are they in such profusion as in the area between Stoodley Pike and the Hebden Water. Every hillside is divided by them into small, rectangular fields, some less than an acre in extent: the allotments of former common land as it was parcelled out under enclosure awards.

Many of the houses date from the late seventeenth and early eighteenth centuries. Solidly built, with squared blocks of gritstone, with mullioned windows and flagstone roofs all a sooty black, they appear dour and forbidding. When they have been newly pointed with their joints picked out in white they look as if specially designed to provide subjects for woodengravers.

About here the Ordnance Survey map indicates a number of wayside crosses, or their former sites. One of them is a mile west of the Pennine Way in a dip in Heptonstall Moor at a height of 1,250 ft. These crosses were alongside routes used by the monks of Whalley Abbey. Some of the tracks are old salt-ways and packhorse ways, and there is still a Packhorse Inn a quarter of a mile down the road from Widdop towards Blake Dean. Hereabouts Halifax Corporation has dammed the feeder streams of Hebden Water to form a chain of reservoirs. The Pennine Way crosses the embankment of one of them, Walshaw Dean Middle Reservoir, to mount to Withins Height. Over the hill the track runs close to the ruins of a farmhouse marked on the map as "Withins". Whether this was the original of Wuthering

Heights; whether Ponden Hall, alongside the Way down in the valley, was Thrushcross Grange; or the Raven Rock, known locally as Ponden Kirk, was the Penistone Crag of Wuthering Heights need not be argued, but here we are in the home country of the Brontë sisters. A detour of three miles will take one into Haworth, to the parsonage where they lived and wrote, and where some of their relics and intimate belongings are gathered in a museum.

From the head of Ponden Reservoir, field paths mount to Crag Bottom, and then less obvious moorland tracks lead to Ickornshaw, the Norsemen's name for Squirrel Wood.

By devious paths, through more small fields, by Middleton, birthplace of Philip Snowden, first Labour Chancellor of the Exchequer, the Way continues to Lothersdale, and then climbs again to Pinhaw Beacon (1,273 ft.). This modest height commands a wide and varied view ranging from Pendle Hill, just over the Lancashire border in the south-west, across the Ribble Valley to the Bowland Fells. To the north-west, Ribblesdale parts Ingleborough and Pen-y-ghent. Then comes the level brow of Fountains Fell, and circling eastwards we see the limestone heights above Malham, then Buckden Pike and Great Whernside at the head of Wharfedale, and Earl's Seat and Simon Seat lower down that valley.

Four miles to the north-east is Skipton, part mill-town and part market-town for Dales farmers, with an ancient castle and imposing church dominating its High Street. Here the River Aire has breached the Pennines, hence the strategic siting of the castle by the Normans. Before them, the gap had been reconnoitred by the Romans who drove a road through it, linking Ribchester in Lancashire with Ilkley and York. Long before Agricola's day, this was an important route used by Bronze Age traders travelling between Ireland and Scandinavia.

Down from Pinhaw there is a transition from the swarthy Elslack Moor to limestone country with green pastures and meadows. For a few hundred yards the

Limestone landscape, near Malham

Way follows the line of the Roman road into Thornton in Craven. Out of that village, Cam Lane leads past the entrance to a huge limestone quarry and northwards over Town Hill to the Leeds and Liverpool Canal. The promoters of this venture announced in 1766, three thousand years or more later than the Bronze Age traders, that "It must be acceptable to the public to be informed that a person with great industry and application has discovered an opening between the mountains of Yorkshire and Lancashire, which is the most eligible, if not the only one, Nature has formed for this important work".

The canal towpath is followed northerly for about three-quarters of a mile, passing under the Skipton-Clitheroe road which is carried by one bridge piled on another. Beyond the next bridge, Williamson Bridge, we short-circuit the canal by field paths leading to Gargrave, between low, elongated hills of boulder clay left by glaciers at the close of the Ice Age.

From Gargrave the Way crosses Eshton Moor and at

the foot of Eel Ark Hill reaches the Aire, which is followed upstream on the west side until Newfield Bridge and then on the east bank, skirting the village of Airton and passing Hanlith Hall on the way to Malham. Half a mile west of the route at Hanlith Bridge is Kirkby Malham, with a fine fifteenth-century church containing a font, possibly Anglian, some Jacobean box-pews and canopied niches carved on the western pillars of the nave. Oliver Cromwell is reputed to have signed the register as witness to three civil weddings when staying with his friend General Lambert at Calton Hall.

If the divergence to Kirkby Malham is made, instead of returning to Hanlith, the Malham road may be followed for 300 yards, then, from a stile on the right, a path leads to the river by Scalegill Mill and on to Malham passing Aire Head Springs. Here a stream emerges after following a subterranean course for three miles from the Water Sinks near Malham Tarn, a reminder that we are now in limestone country, where streams play hide and seek, carving out caverns some of which are still "measureless to man".

Yellow tormentil (*Potentilla erecta*)

CHAPTER FOUR

Malham to Swaledale

Airedale, as a valley, is terminated abruptly by an up-standing scar of limestone in which, on approaching Malham from the south, we see the upper part of the precipitous wall of Malham Cove and, a mile east of it, a notch in the skyline marking the great cleft of Gordale Scar. This latter feature, a narrow gorge with sheer and over-hanging walls, once an underground cavern but now roofless, lies east of the Pennine Way, but should not on that account be missed.

On the outskirts of Malham, a field path leads to Malham Cove, now seen in full stature as a soaring cliff of limestone cut back in an arc, almost an amphitheatre. The stream emerging from the base of the Cove has followed an underground course from near the old smelt mill, one and a half miles to the north-west.

East of the stream there are some well-marked lynchets or cultivation terraces made by Anglian farmers a thousand years or more ago. Still earlier inhabitants have also left their mark, for the path which mounts to the western edge of the Cove crosses an Iron Age settlement with low ridges indicating the ancient field boundaries.

On top of the Cove is a platform or pavement of large blocks of limestone, separated by crevices, some of which are several feet deep. In a bygone age a stream flowing from Malham Tarn poured over the lip of the Cove. Now the valley is bone dry, for the stream disappears at the Water Sinks, a mile to the north, only to surface again at Aire Head below Malham village.

The Cove, and the whole escarpment of which it is a part, are consequences of the Craven Faults, compound, dislocated fractures, as it were, of the very bones of the earth, whereby the strata have been broken across so that rocks, which should be relatively higher than the limestone, are brought down to its level or even lower. The total displacement of the faults is estimated to exceed 5,000 feet.

From the edge of the Cove (but not too near the precipitous drop) the effect on the landscape of the Mid-

Craven Fault is very pronounced. South of the escarpment the lighter green of the limestone grassland gives way to marshy ground with coarse bent grass and rushes, or to heather and bracken, typical vegetation of the Yoredale Shales and Millstone Grit. Even the stone walls mark the approximate line of the fault, for their builders used the materials nearest to hand: limestone north of the fault, and gritstone on the south side.

The Dry Valley may be followed northwards, but the Pennine Way runs more to the east along a depression known locally as Trougate or Troughgate. This crosses Prior Rakes, once a pasture of Bolton Priory in Wharfedale.

The long, level brow of Fountains Fell, now visible, is a reminder that Fountains Abbey also owned land hereabouts as well as the fishing rights in Malham Tarn. From the thirteenth century until the Reformation, most of this district was held by the monasteries of Bolton and Fountains.

As we approach Malham Tarn another change in the vegetation, from smooth turf, perhaps starred with yellow mountain pansies *(Viola lutea)*, to rough, tufty grass, marks the crossing of the North Craven Fault. The Tarn rests here on a floor of Silurian Slates, which owing to the fault are higher instead of being considerably lower than the limestone to the south.

The Tarn, the adjacent land and Malham Tarn House now belong to the National Trust, but the house is leased to the Field Studies Council who use it as one of their centres for residential courses in a wide range of countryside subjects. Here many famous Victorians were entertained, including Thomas Hughes, Charles Darwin, John Ruskin and Charles Kingsley. Evidence of Kingsley's visit will be found in *The Water Babies* in the description of Lowthwaite Crag (Malham Cove) and Vendale (Littondale).

After rounding the Tarn, and passing behind the Field Study Centre, the Way turns north to climb Fountains

Great Shunner Fell, from Gaudy House, above Gayle

Fell where, for the first time since leaving Derbyshire, we rise to 2,000 feet. The track to the summit, now grassed over, was once well trodden by packhorses carrying poor quality coal mined here early in the last century. Over the top the track descends to the Halton Gill road at Blishmire Close, but the Pennine Way cuts a corner to Peter Castle, an impressive name for some old sheep folds.

Pen-y-ghent, which was seen broadside on from Fountains Fell, now presents a more striking profile. Churn Milk Hole, beyond Dale Head Farm, is a reminder that we are in pot-holing country, where the caves and passages with which the limestone pedestals of Ingleborough and Pen-y-ghent are riddled, are much frequented by enthusiastic pot-holers.

A cairn marks the Way across a short stretch of moor to a drystone wall which is then followed as it mounts the sharp nose of Pen-y-ghent to the summit (2,273 ft.), one of the best viewpoints on the Pennine Way. Pendle Hill, over the Lancashire border, is prominent in the south and a little nearer on the other side of the Ribble Valley are the Bowland Fells.

Almost due west is Ingleborough (2,373 ft.), with its flat cap of gritstone which makes it recognisable from afar. Farther north is the higher, but less imposing, Whernside (2,419 ft.).

To include the three peaks, Pen-y-ghent, Ingleborough and Whernside in a day's walk was long considered a creditable feat, but nowadays stalwarts start from Kettlewell in Wharfedale, and cover six or seven peaks before descending from Whernside into Dentdale.

On the upper slopes of Pen-y-ghent, in June and July, may be seen the white flowers of the cloud berry *(Rubus chamaemorus),* which towards the end of August have matured into orange-coloured berries. But the chief glory of Pen-y-ghent is the purple mountain saxifrage *(Saxifraga oppositifolia),* which flourishes in April. From June onwards the yellow mountain saxifrage *(Saxifraga aizoides)* may be found in the neighbourhood of Hunt Pot.

A broken-down wall rings Hunt Pot, the mouth of which is a rift about twenty feet long and six feet wide. Into this black cleft a moorland stream plunges to a depth of nearly 200 feet and emerges at Brants Gill Head down in the valley. A wall running west and then north-west leads to a shooters' cabin at the end of a walled lane leading to Horton in Ribblesdale, but, before descending, it is well worth while walking about 300 yards in the opposite direction, to Hull Pot. When in spate a river there makes a spectacular fall of sixty feet into a large rectangular chasm about 60 yards long and 15 yards wide.

Horton is an unpretentious, scattered village marred

by extensive limestone quarries which, fortunately, do not interfere with the fine prospect of Pen-y-ghent rising in two concave sweeps from a limestone platform, parcelled by drystone walls into rectangular allotments.

The parish church, with a square sixteenth-century tower and a roof of lead (traditionally mined near Hull Pot) appears as sturdy as its background. The south door displays Norman chevron decoration and the font is Early Norman.

The cylindrical pillars and round arches of the nave are out of perpendicular, as if the structure had been tilted slightly to the south. The church is floored with blue Horton flags, a reminder that the Ribble has cut down through the limestone to the very roots of the Pennines. At Coombs Quarry there is a famous text-book illustration of horizontal beds of limestone resting on highly inclined Silurian flagstones.

From the Crown Inn at Horton, the Way follows an old green lane once used by the monks of Jervaulx in Wensleydale, who bred horses at Horton. We leave this track on Birkwith Moor to join, at Old Ing, another grass track, once an important packhorse road, as is evident from an inscription on a little gritstone bridge carrying the road over Cam Beck at Ling Gill. The inscription, now barely decipherable, reads, "Anno 1765. This bridge was repaired at the charge of the whole West Rideing".

Below the bridge the stream plunges down a tree-fringed ravine, its narrow floor strewn with huge blocks of water-worn limestone. It is possible to enter the Gill at its foot and walk up the stream bed. Only thus can one fully appreciate the beauty of this impressive gorge which affords shelter to a luxuriant vegetation.

On Cam End the Pennine Way joins a Roman road, now a grass-grown track running along a ledge of the fell. Down on the right is a swarthy, moor-rimmed bowl from which headstreams of Wharfe and Ribble make sluggish beginnings, one to reach, via the Ouse, the North Sea, and the other, flowing westwards, the Irish Sea.

Hidden from the road are the two lonely and now

untenanted farms of Cam Houses where, when the track was more frequented, a gun was fired at nightfall to guide belated travellers. At Bainbridge, down in Wensleydale, to which the Roman road leads, a horn was sounded for the same purpose, as it still is as a matter of custom in the winter months.

At Kidhow Gate we leave the Roman road for a pleasant, grass track along a shoulder of Dodd Fell with the deep, narrow valley of Snaizeholme on the left. Given a clear day, Kidhow Gate is an excellent viewpoint. Pen-y-ghent peeps over High Green Field Knott, and Ingleborough and Whernside are still prominent. In the north-west the domed Howgill Fells block the foot of Dentdale and beyond them the Lakeland hills may be in view. Slightly west of north, Wild Boar Fell dips its sharp nose into the defile of Mallerstang. East of it and more distant, Cross Fell may be identified by its level brow and the rounded tops of its neighbours, Little and Great Dun Fells.

Eastward is the narrow valley of Upper Wharfedale, or Langstrothdale to give it its ancient name, bounded by green hillsides with thin strips of woodland and grey limestone terraces. These, in July, may be gilded with a profusion of yellow rockroses *(Helianthemum chamae-cistus)*. On the higher ground the walled pastures merge into the brown moorland of Buckden Pike (2,302 feet) and Great Whernside (2,310 feet), so named to distinguish it from its neighbour, Little Whernside, not from *the* Whernside which is more than a hundred feet higher.

Followed to the end, the track along Dodd Fell offers an easy descent to the Widdale road a mile east of Hawes, but the Pennine Way turns over Ten End to drop down to the hamlet of Gayle and thence by stone-flagged field paths to Hawes.

On this descent there is a fine prospect of Wensleydale, the widest, smoothest and most verdant of the Dales—a glacier-gouged trough in the hills which centuries of cultivation have clothed with a green serenity. Unlike the other dales, it takes its name from the village of Wensley and not from its river, the Ure.

Hawes, the market town of the upper dale, is a small 41

unpretentious place, with a wide market place narrowing like a funnel to a cobbled street winding between stone-built houses. The church is little more than a century old but it is on record that Richard III appointed a priest to the chapel here in 1483.

A bus service links the villages of the dale and with its aid, before continuing northwards, one can visit the falls at Aysgarth, the ruins of Bolton Castle where Mary Queen of Scots was imprisoned for six months, and the shell of Middleham Castle where Warwick the Kingmaker lived in lavish splendour when, we are told, "six oxen were eaten at breakfast".

Before climbing out of Wensleydale, Hardrow Force must be seen. You pay a small charge at the Green Dragon and go through the back door and along a path into a dell where the beck plunges over a limestone ledge into a pool a hundred feet below. Black shale glistening with spray has been cut back under the limestone so that one may walk behind the waterfall. In former days there was a bandstand here and thousands came to the annual band contests. One year the famous Blondin crossed the ravine on a tightrope, stopping half-way to cook an omelette.

Great Shunner Fell thrusts a convenient spur southwards between Cotterdale and the valley of the Hearne Beck. A track starting by the village school at Hardrow leads up to this spur by which the Pennine Way ascends to the summit of Great Shunner (2,340 ft.[1]).

From Humesett Beacon there is a fine backward view of Upper Wensleydale. The Pennine trio Whernside, Ingleborough and Pen-y-ghent are still in view. The line of the Way descending from Ten End may be picked out, and east of it the road climbing steeply from Gayle up the side of the Wether Fell appears to be standing on end. Lower down the dale the rock-fringed cap of Addlebrough and the domed crest of Penhill are prominent. Humesett Beacon is one of the innumerable cairns on Great Shunner, presumably built by shepherds, but why no one seems to know. Many of them are marked on the

[1] See page 93 for escape route.

East Stonesdale, Upper Swaledale

map either as beacons, curricks or curracks. This last word is derived from the Welsh *carreg,* a pile of stones.

North-west of the summit is Hugh Seat, named after Sir Hugh de Morville, who took part in the murder of Thomas Becket.

An easterly and then south-easterly course along the watershed towards Lovely Seat will lead to the top of the Buttertubs Pass, so named from the limestone pot-holes on the Swaledale side of the Pass. This means, however, a two-mile descent to Thwaite on a road carrying considerable motor traffic in summer.

Rougher walking, but decidedly more interesting, is the approved route which swings round the head of

Stock Dale and on the descent to Thwaite gives a superb view of Swaledale: from its uppermost reaches to the rounded height of Kidson with Rogan's Seat (2,203 ft.) in the background and down dale to the limestone scars of Fremington Edge above Reeth, where Arkengarthdale joins the main valley.

Swaledale is much narrower than Wensleydale: the hillsides are steeper, so steep that one wonders how the hayfields are ever mown. A winding valley with the river, unlike the Ure, almost always in the picture, it is more diversified than Wensleydale and, despite considerable tourist traffic, seemingly less concerned with the outer world.

Curlew

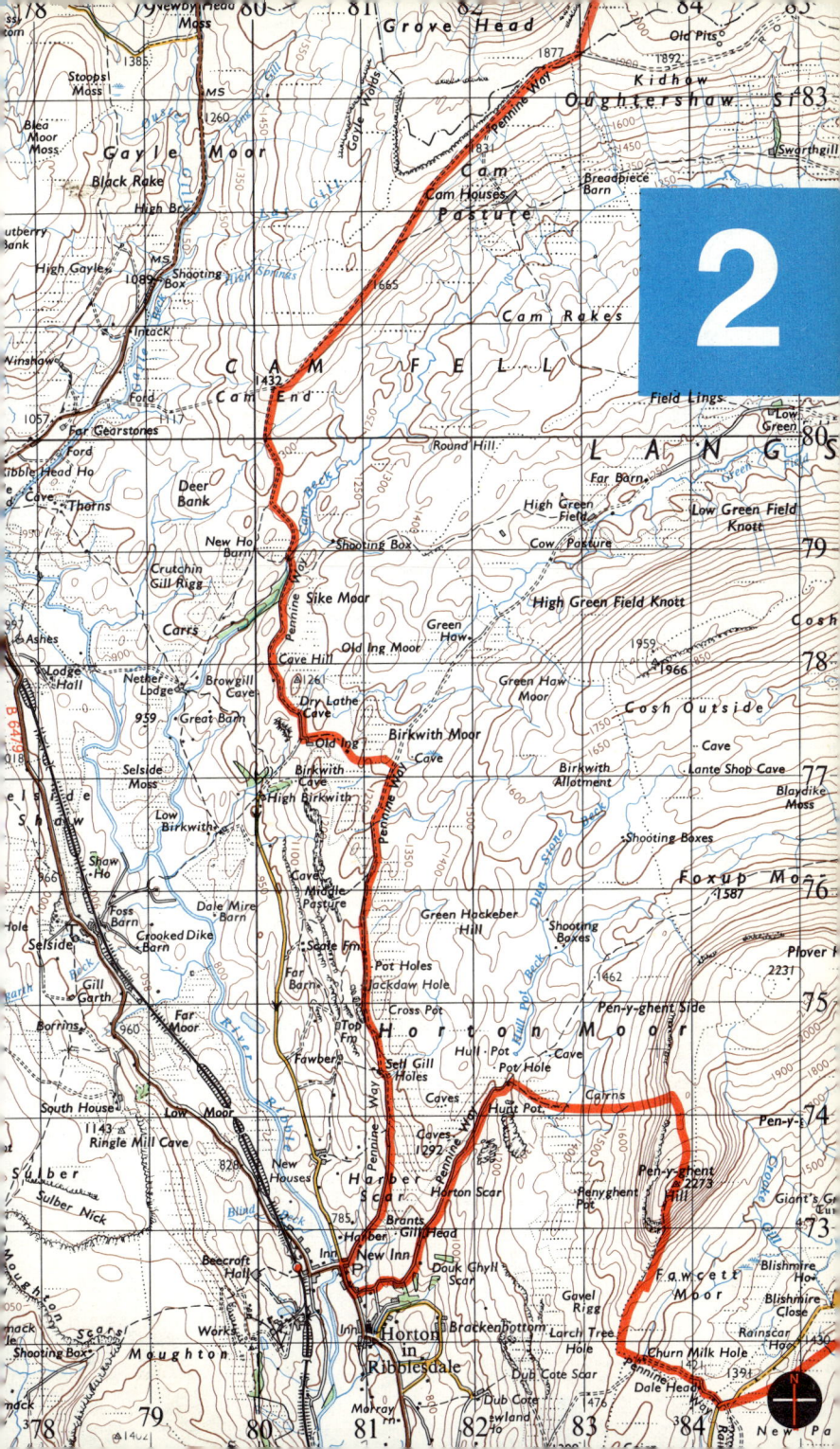

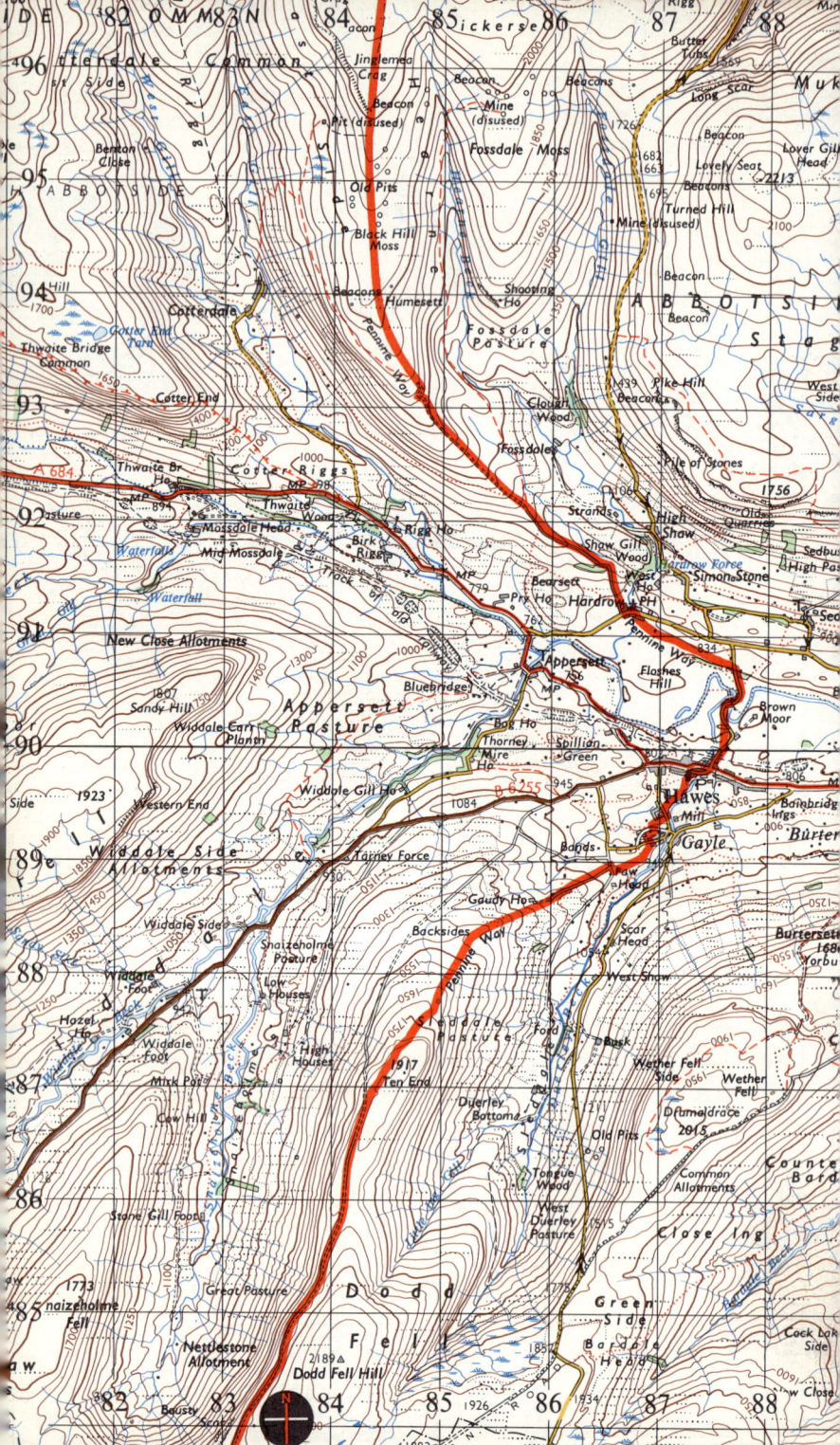

CHAPTER FIVE

Swaledale to Tynedale

Thwaite, to which the Way descends from Great Shunner Fell, is a huddle of sturdy, grey houses built from doorsteps to roof tops and square chimneys of local stone. The name, meaning a clearing, is a reminder of the Norsemen, who settled here a thousand years ago, and to whom we are indebted for many of the place names. The common elements like fell, scar, gill and garth are all of Old Norse origin. Hawes is a different version of Hause, as in Esk Hause in the Lake District, and means a neck or col between two valleys.

The Old Norse *saetr* appears in Appersett and Burtersett in Wensleydale and in Gunnerside in Swaledale. In these instances it meant a shieling or hill pasture, e.g., Gunnar's Shieling. Lovely Seat, Rogan's Seat, Raven Seat and similar names are from the same root.

Almost every field in Upper Swaledale has another reminder of those early settlers in the form of a stone-built barn, known as a lathe from the Scandinavian *Hlatha*. These buildings, usually on the higher part of the field, are of two storeys, a byre for cattle on the ground, and a hayloft above.

"Men of Suadale", Leland wrote, "were much used in digging lead ore." Lead was, in fact, mined here by the Romans, and for nearly two hundred years, down to the latter part of the last century, the mining of it was a prosperous industry employing at one time more than three thousand men, and producing 40,000 tons of lead yearly. All that remains of those days are roofless ruins, old shafts and adits, and here and there a smelt-mill chimney or an artificial ravine known as a "hush", made in prospecting for lead. A stream was sometimes dammed to form a reservoir and when a sufficient head of water was obtained, the dam was broken and the rush of water tearing down the hillside would sweep away loose earth and possibly uncover a vein of lead.

The famous naturalist brothers Richard and Cherry Kearton were born at Thwaite, a fact commemorated on the wall of the little school which serves Thwaite and the nearby village of Muker.

From Thwaite the Way mounts to the farm of Kisdon and then rounds the east side of the hill. There is a track on the west side, the old Corpse Road, along which in medieval days funeral processions made their way, drawing the corpse on a sled at the start of the journey from Keld to the nearest consecrated ground at Grinton, twelve miles down the dale. To take that way to Keld would, however, mean missing the deep and narrow gorge the Swale has çarved between Kisdon and the lower buttresses of Rogan's Seat, and also missing Kisdon Force where the river plunges in two foaming leaps over limestone ledges finely framed between grey crags and wooded hillsides. Near Keld a Pennine Way sign points downhill to a wooden bridge over the Swale. A little nearer the village a barn carries the cryptic inscription "IADARA, 1687", said to be the initials of I., D., and R. Alderson, a name still common in the district.

Keld lies in a hollow almost hidden from the road. On the road there is a chapel, a tall shooting lodge, now a youth hostel, a house, once the post office and village shop, and, facing down dale towards Thwaite and Great Shunner Fell, a large house formerly the Cat Hole Inn, once famed for its hospitality but now a private residence. Down in the village proper, rough steps lead to Catrake Force where the river when in spate roars over rock ledges into a swirling pool of peaty-brown water.

After crossing the above-mentioned wooden bridge, near a small waterfall on East Gill Beck, the Way mounts sharply by East Stonesdale Farm and continues on a track shown on the Ordnance Survey 1 Inch map as ending below High Frith Farm, but which, in fact, continues across Lad Gill and up to Tan Hill. Here, 1,732 feet above sea-level, is the highest pub in England, a gaunt, white-washed house with adjacent buildings which are falling into ruin. Nowadays the inn is much visited by motorists; in its earlier days it served the pedlars, miners and those from round about who came with horses and carts for a load of poor quality coal.

The thin seams of coal are known to have been worked in the thirteenth century and mining on a small scale lingered until the 1930s. Fortunately a proposal to start open-cast mining in 1958 was not allowed.

Behind the inn, cut in the bedrock by no skilled hand, is the following inscription:

IN
MEMORY OF
SUSAN PEACOCK TANHILL
WHO DIED 24 MAY, 1937
LIVED HERE
FROM 1902

She was a well-known hostess who could be warmly hospitable or bluntly outspoken: ready, according to her whim, to gossip or tell one plainly that it was time to be moving.

Tan Hill commands a wide view across Stainmore's great spread of moorland surging up to the swell and long ridge of Mickle Fell (2,591 ft.), the highest hill in Yorkshire.

Through the gap of Stainmore a glacier carried boulders of Shap granite from Westmorland right across to the Tees mouth, and down the Yorkshire coast as far as Robin Hood's Bay. There is evidence that the gap was used by Bronze Age traders and inevitably the Romans discovered it. Agricola made a road through it, branching from Dere Street, now the Great North Road, at Scotch Corner and linking York and Carlisle. In recent years there has been discovered a series of signal stations by which messages were conveyed perhaps by semaphores between the headquarters at York and the fort at Stanwix near Carlisle.

A cairned track leads down to join the moor road to Sleightholme. Thence, after crossing Sleightholme Beck by a wooden bridge anchored against floods by a stout chain, a path leads to Trough Heads and across the moor to West Mellwater and God's Bridge, where the River Greta runs underneath a bed of limestone and so provides a natural bridge.

Bowes,[1] two and a half miles to the east, offers accommodation for those who do not fancy walking the 22 miles from Keld to Middleton in Teesdale in one day.

The Roman road over Stainmore was defended by stations at Brough in the west and at Bowes in the east, where the fort, covering some four acres, was known as *Lavatrae*. Within the boundaries of the fort there are the ruins of a Norman castle with a massive rectangular keep. The nearby church, probably contemporary with the castle, retains some Norman work. In the north transept there is a stone with a Roman dedication from which the name of Caesar Publius Septimus Geta was erased after he had been murdered by his brother and joint emperor, Caracalla: obliterations on such inscriptions were made throughout the empire by Caracalla's order.

In the south-east part of the churchyard is the gravestone of George Ashton Taylor, which Dickens said put the idea of Smike into his mind. At the western edge of the village a long building, now a café, proudly proclaims itself the Dotheboys Hall of *Nicholas Nickleby*.

The direct line of the Pennine Way from God's Bridge passes under the railway from Barnard Castle to Kirkby Stephen (once the highest railway in England but now closed) and after crossing the Bowes Moor road rises to Ravock Castle, the ruins of a shepherd's hut, descends to a foot bridge over Deepdale Beck and climbs again alongside a wall by the hummocky moraine mounds of Knotts Hills to Race Yate Rigg.

From this point Mickle Fell fills the view north-westerly. Nearer at hand is the flat-topped Shacklesborough (1,489 ft.) like a small Ingleborough, and north-easterly is the rocky crest of Goldsborough (1,274 ft.). Away to the south-east the abrupt northern termination of the Cleveland Hills is in sight. Southwards stretches the great waste of Stainmore with Tan Hill still visible and beyond it the heights from the level brow of Great Shunner Fell to Nine Standards Rigg. From the gate in the boundary fence on Race Yate, a cairn gives the line

God's Bridge, River Greta, Stainmore

for the descent to Clove Lodge Farm. Thence more discernible tracks lead round the head of Blackton Reservoir in Baldersdale, over Hunderthwaite Moor to Grassholme Reservoir in Lunedale, and by Wythes Hill to Middleton in Teesdale.

This large village was formerly a lead-mining centre. The London Lead Company, a Quaker concern, early in the eighteenth century obtained from the Commissioners of Greenwich Hospital mining leases in the Alston district, and later extended their operations into Teesdale where they made their headquarters at Middleton. The company opened up many new mines, built houses, schools and chapels and made roads into the hills, most of which are now grass-grown and almost forgotten. An exception is the road up Teesdale from

53

Middleton, mounting to 1,962 feet on Yad Moss before descending to Alston.

A change from moorland tramping is the riverside walk on the Yorkshire bank of the Tees from Middleton Bridge to High Force. The Tees befits its name, said to mean "boiling or surging river". Often the peaty-brown waters are churned to cream and amber foam and with blue sky and white clouds overhead give a kaleidoscopic effect of every conceivable hue.

Upstream is a wide valley with grey-green hillsides dotted with white-washed farmhouses rising up to more than 2,000 feet to the watershed between Teesdale and Weardale. On the west the heights are more sombre and steep, from Holwick Fell by the conical Noon Hill to the sharp-nosed Cronkley Fell.

At Wynch Bridge the bed of the river narrows and the river rushes swiftly over an outcrop of the Whin Sill forming the fall known as Low Force. Farther upstream, at High Force, the Tees has cut back a gorge and makes a leap of some seventy feet between massive bastions of Whin Sill resting on beds of limestone and shale. The more usual approach to the fall is on the Durham bank. For this one should cross Holwick Head Bridge and turn up the road to High Force Hotel. A toll of 3d. allows one to follow a gravel path through pine woods to the foot of the fall, where the foaming water thunders down into a dark, swirling pool. On the right a flight of rough steps leads to the top of the fall.

On the Yorkshire side of the river such a close approach to the fall is not possible, but this is more than compensated for by the better impression one gets of the gorge and of the setting of the fall in relation to the landscape.

After seventy miles in Yorkshire, first in the West Riding and then in the North Riding, the Pennine Way crosses the Tees by Cronkley Bridge into Durham. Next the Harwood Beck is crossed and a track followed to the unoccupied Widdybank Farm where the Tees winds

between Widdybank Fell and the northern spur of Cronkley Fell.

A "widdy", it is said locally, was a slate pencil. The English Dialect Dictionary gives no mention of this, but the Ordnance Survey 6 Inch map names a ruined building as "pencil mill", and a small inlier of Skiddaw Slates was formerly quarried there.

Hereabouts the mealy primrose *(Primula farinosa)* flourishes and despite the depredations of thoughtless visitors the blue gentian *(Gentiana verna)* still blooms on Widdybank Fell.

Upstream, round the thrusting shoulder of Cronkley Fell, is Holmwath, a Norse name meaning "island ford". Next the Way winds between boulders fallen from the crags of Falcon Clints and up to the foot of Caldron Snout where the Tees comes cascading some hundred and fifty feet down a natural and uneven stairway of dark rocks of the Whin Sill. From ledge to ledge the Way mounts besides the fuming, leaping water.

Above Caldron Snout the Tees formerly flowed lazily through a wide moorland waste. Now it is impounded in the Cow Green reservoir, the building of which was vigorously but vainly opposed by the naturalist and amenity societies. Above the fall, the Way enters Westmorland, and follows a rough and boggy track to the isolated farms at Birkdale. Beyond the upper house, after crossing Grain Beck, a track mounts to a cairn by some old mine buildings marked on the map as "Moss Shop". These "shops", of which there are many on the hills, were places where the lead miners lived during their working week, cooked their own food and slept on straw-filled bunks.

This part of the Pennine Way from Teesdale to the Eden Valley is the wildest and loneliest crossing in the whole length of the Pennines. Swarthy, shaggy moorlands rise on either hand to more than 2,000 feet and after two hours' walking westwards from Birkdale there seems no end to the wilderness. Having left Maize Beck[2] where it swings northwards, we walk across a level

[2] For additional notes on this section of the Way, see page 93

plain with limestone peeping through the green turf, particularly noticeable after the dark peat and heather and the wiry bents. Then with dramatic suddenness we reach High Cup Nick and look down a horseshoe cleft in the Pennine escarpment fringed with 80-foot columnar crags of the Whin Sill. Six or seven hundred feet below, a thin wisp of a stream winds down High Cup Gill leading the eye to the wide, lush vale of the Eden, where pastures, meadows and cornfields are divided by hedgerows, instead of the drystone walls of the fells. Beyond this vari-coloured chequerboard are the Lake District hills ranging from Skiddaw to Coniston Old Man.

Round the north side of the Gill, first on a cairned path and then by a stony farm road, the Way descends the abrupt western edge of the Pennines, which is better appreciated from farther west. There it appears in some lights as a dusky blue wall rising sheer above the Eden Valley where the ploughed fields are tinged with the red of the Permian and Triassic sandstones.

Here, as in the Malham district, the escarpment is due to a fault system, in this instance giving a displacement of more than 7,000 feet.

During the descent one cannot fail to notice the line of conical hills at the foot of the escarpment, including Murton Pike, Dufton Pike, and Knock Pike. These consist of pre-Carboniferous rocks—Skiddaw Slates and Borrowdale Volcanic rocks which have been thrust up along the fractures of the fault system.

By way of "Mexico" and Town Head, Dufton is reached—an open, alluring village ranged round a wide green, its houses built of local red sandstone, some lime-washed white, cream or pale blue, most of them with windows, door posts and corner stones painted chocolate-brown. In the background is the conical Dufton Pike. More distant are the flat cap of Cross Fell and the rounded crests of its lesser neighbours Little and Great Dun Fells, the latter crowned with radar masts.

They tell in Dufton of the ferocity of the helm wind which sometimes blows down from Cross Fell with such violence, they say, as to overturn carts, uproot trees and lift the roofs off farm buildings. When the wind is blowing, a bank of cloud, known as the "helm", lies on, or just above, the summit of the fell. Three or four miles to the south-west there is another line of cloud known as the "bar". Meteorologists say the phenomenon is due to cold air from the east pouring down the hillside. At the lower levels it warms up and begins to rise again. Professor Gordon Manley, who made a study of the climate of Cross Fell (*Climate and The British Scene*, p. 48) says the escarpment "acts like a submerged weir in a stream of water; a standing wave is set up just below the weir. . . . The clear sky between helm and bar is associated with the descending air; where the air again reaches the same level as the helm, cloud is again present as the bar".

The helm wind may have given Cross Fell its earlier name of Fiends Fell—there is still a Fiends Fell a few miles farther north, overlooking the Penrith-Alston road at Hartside Cross. *The Place Names of Cumberland* (p. 243) says: "It is probable that the cross from which the modern name is derived was erected in order to give a Christian association to a mountain under the influence of evil powers." Tradition, less trammelled by needs of precision, credits St. Augustine with banishing the fiends though there is no record that he ever travelled so far north.

The building of the radar station on Great Dun Fell led to the metalling of the old mine road up Knock Ore Gill and a consequent diversion of the Pennine Way up Swindale Beck and over Knock Fell (2,604 ft.) and thence to the head of Knock Ore Gill. There a stony track, remains of one of the London Lead Company's mine roads, goes off eastwards into the head of Teesdale and thence into South Tynedale. The Pennine Way strikes northward, skirting the radar station on Great Dun Fell, then over Little Dun Fell, and down to a wire fence marking the Cumberland-Westmorland boundary. Beyond a boggy hollow, draining on one hand to the

View from High Cup Nick,
across the Eden Valley to the Lake District hills

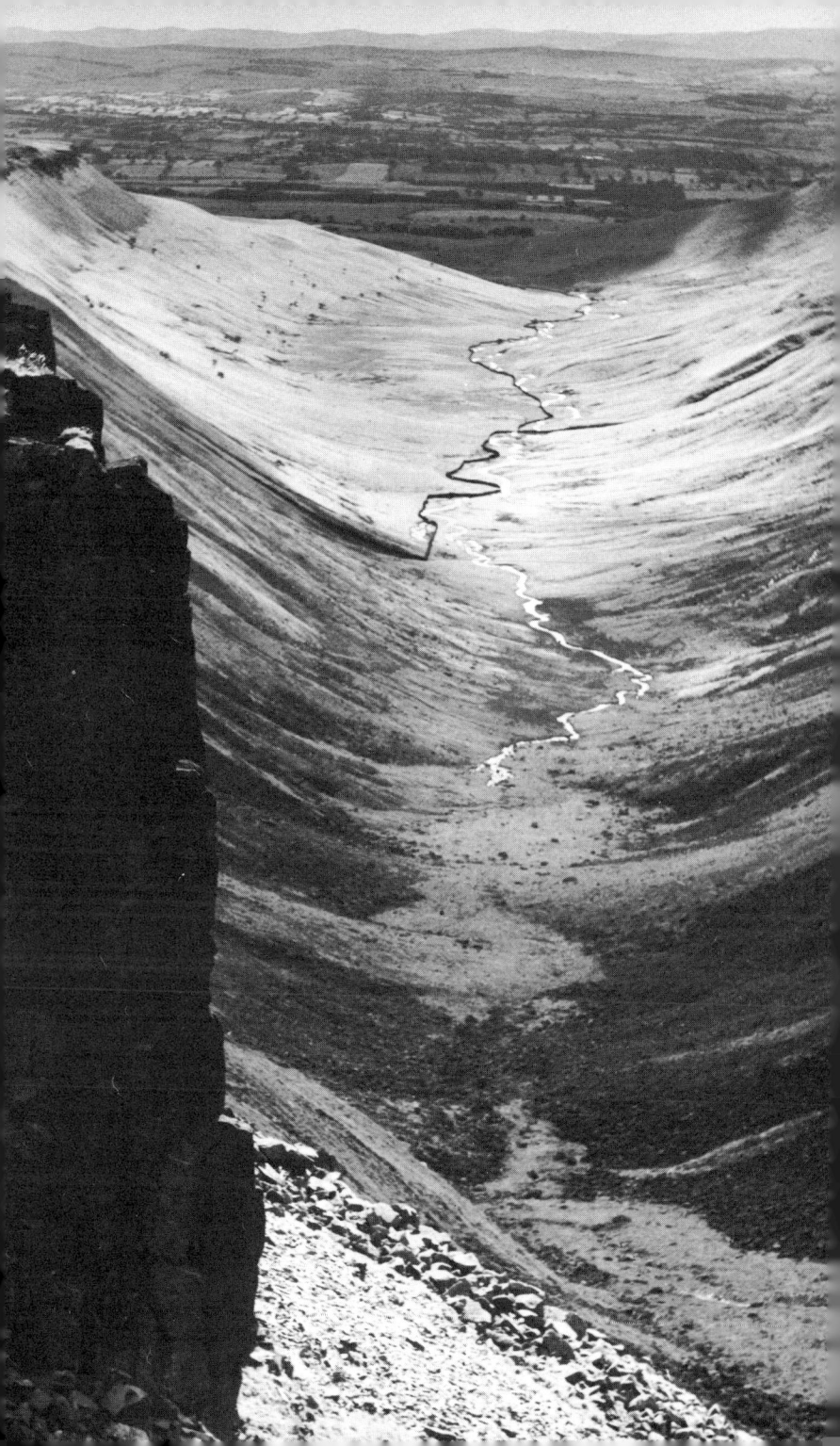

Tees and on the other to Crowdundle Beck and the Eden, a rise of 400 feet leads to the summit of Cross Fell (2,930 ft.),[3] the highest point on the Pennine Way and commanding the most far-flung view in the whole journey. Given a clear day, it is an interesting exercise to distinguish the different heights in the Lake District. Saddleback is easy to recognise by its hollowed crest from which it takes its name. North of it, Skiddaw overlooks the Mungrisdale Fells. Through the gap south of Saddleback, Grisedale Pike and the Grassmoor Fells may be recognised. South again the series of Dodds lead the eye to Helvellyn. More distant, the pointed crest of Bow Fell may be identified in the gap of Grisedale. A gleam of Ullswater may give a clue to the long line of High Street, leading to the conical Ill Bell.

South-south-east, Wild Boar Fell is prominent above the defile of Mallerstang. West of it are the rounded tops of the Howgill Fells and south of it the three peaks of Whernside, Ingleborough and Pen-y-ghent. In the north-west, beyond the Solway Firth, Criffel and the Galloway Hills are in view. A good fifty miles away in the north-east, and almost at the end of the Pennine Way, Cheviot stands well above the neighbouring heights.

The imperceptible, highest point of the Cross Fell plateau is marked by a large cairn with an Ordnance Survey concrete post nearby. Here in 1832 (when political enthusiasm must have been greater than today) a crowd gathered with fifty brass bands to celebrate the passing of the Reform Bill.

From the summit two small cairns are aligned in the direction of the descent. From the farther of these, a third pile marks the way to a fourth and larger cairn at the eastern edge of a fringe of boulders. A few yards down to the left from this cairn is the source of Kirkland Beck, a spring marked on the Ordnance Survey maps as Crossfell Well. This was formerly known as Gentleman's Well and is still so called by elderly local people.

T. Sopwith, writing on mining in the district in 1833, described an ascent of Cross Fell: "A little after sun-

[3] For additional notes, see page 96.

Dufton and, in background, Cross Fell

rise", he tells, "the air being very cold and piercing, we struck our tent and formed with it a screen to the windward of a large stone flag, which we raised for a table, and placed stone seats around. After partaking of an excellent breakfast, we repaired to Gentleman's Well; here we washed and dressed, and after packing up our superfluous clothing, made by active exercise a gradual transition from the cold of a Cross-Fell night to the increasing warmth of a burning midsummer day."

The stone slab and seats in a roughly walled enclosure may still be seen close by the Well. Below this point a few cairns mark the way to a track, said to be an old corpse way, linking Garrigill in the east with Kirkland on the west. In bad weather the shortest way to lower ground is the one westwards to Kirkland, but do not be beguiled that way in search of the Hanging Walls of Mark Anthony at Ranbeck. The name on the map is said to be the only Roman feature of what are probably natural mounds.

Eastwards the Pennine Way follows the track, which passes old mine workings and crosses feeders of the Black Burn as it approaches the disused Cashwell Mine. On the tips here may be found fragments of gleaming lead ore (galena), lumps of barytes (pick one up and you will know why miners called it heavy spar) and yellow or blue fluorspar; the latter variety is the Blue John which at the southern end of the Way they will tell you is found only in Derbyshire.

From Cashwell Mine the track is well marked for the four-mile descent to Garrigill. This is a quiet hamlet, partly strung along the stream of the South Tyne and partly fringing a village green. Here you may find welcome at the George and Dragon or you may continue for another four miles by riverside paths to Alston.

Red Grouse

CHAPTER SIX

Tynedale to Cheviot

Alston consists mainly of a narrow, cobbled street hanging on a steep hillside, a thousand feet above sea-level: a street flanked with stone-built, stone-roofed houses, some with crow-stepped gables and others with stone steps up to their doors. The pillared market cross in the stone-paved market square, which is anything but square, is a reminder of the days when Alston claimed to be the highest market town in England. It was long the centre of a prosperous lead-mining area. In 1233, a Royal Charter granted protection to the miners of Alderston, and in 1350 the mines were managed by a German from Cologne.

This industry led to the Cumberland boundary overstepping the Pennines so that the mining royalties could be collected jointly with those of the Lake District.

The Radcliffe family made a fortune out of the Alston mines and James II made the head of the family Earl of Derwentwater. The last Earl was beheaded for his part in the 1715 Jacobite rising. His estates were confiscated and the mines and mining rights conferred on the Commissioners of Greenwich Hospital.

From Alston Bridge the Pennine Way follows a track to Harbut Lodge. Then, after crossing the road B6292, it rises by Wanwood Bent to join the Maiden Way, a Roman road which was driven over the Pennines from Kirkby Thore in the Eden Valley to join at Carvoran the Roman road now known as the Stanegate.

For the next nine miles the Pennine Way follows the general direction, but not always the exact line, of the Maiden Way, descending for a start to the Gilderdale Burn where we step into Northumberland. Thence the Maiden Way is mapped running south of Whitley Castle, but our route goes to the north of this Roman station, which covered nearly nine acres and which still retains conspicuous earthen ramparts.

From Whitley Castle the Way descends to the hamlet

of Kirkhaugh, the kirk of which is on the far side of the Tyne. Beyond Lintley there is a riverside path for half a mile; then, after a quarter of a mile of road work to the edge of Slaggyford, the route climbs a little, crosses the Knar Burn and the Thinhope Burn and runs along the slopes of Glendue Fell to the Glendue Burn. It will be noticed we are now in the land of burns as distinct from the becks farther south. The last-mentioned stream was formerly named Glen Dhu and Professor E. Ekwall derives the name from the Welsh "glyn", a valley, and "du", black. The stream is shown on the map as draining from a height named Butt of Blackburn. As it descends to the Glendue Burn the Maiden Way is plain to see as a dark band of heather fringed with paler moor grass. Hereabouts the Pennines are declining to the Tyne-Solway Gap beyond which, to the north-east, are the heights of the Whin Sill crowned by Hadrian's Wall.

Once again the road B6292 is crossed and then the Maiden Way, now a metalled road, is left for a less direct route over Hartleyburn Common (north side) and Wain Rigg.

After crossing the Newcastle-Carlisle road, A69, we descend and make our first contact with the ancient frontier of the Roman Empire. This is a fitting place to say a little about that great fortification which we shall follow from Thirlwall to Housesteads.

As we have travelled northwards we have noted the Roman roads through the Aire Gap and over Stainmore. Another road, the Stanegate, ran from Corbridge on the Tyne to Carlisle. These and other roads were made by Julius Agricola, the Roman Governor of Britain, who by A.D. 84 or 85 had conquered northern England and southern Scotland and built a system of strategic roads and forts. In the early part of the second century the conquerors had to abandon their hold on Scotland and withdraw to the line of the Stanegate, and the Emperor Hadrian, who visited Britain in A.D. 122, ordered the building of a wall across the narrow neck of England from Newcastle to Solway Firth. When completed the Wall reached from Wallsend on Tyne to Bowness on Solway, a distance of 73 miles, or 80 Roman miles.

The Wall was probably about 15 feet high with a parapet taking it six feet higher. Along the Wall there were 17 forts built to a common pattern. Between these, at every Roman mile, there was a small fort or barracks called a milecastle, with accommodation for about 50 men and with gateways wide enough to allow wheeled traffic to pass through the Wall. Between each milecastle there were two turrets which served as signalling towers.

The Wall with its forts and ancillary buildings was, though, only one feature of this frontier.

On the north side of the Wall, except where it ran along the tops of crags or by the sea, there was a ditch averaging about 27 feet in width and nine in depth. South of the Wall was an earthwork known as the *vallum*. This was a ditch 20 feet wide and ten feet deep with a flat bottom eight feet wide. Set back from the ditch 30 feet on each side was a mound 20 feet wide.

The *vallum,* unlike the Wall, was not plotted to take advantage of the ground, but was laid out in a series of straight lengths and, consequently, diverging from the Wall in places, occasionally to a distance of half a mile. The *vallum,* says Professor Ian A. Richmond, "turns out to be a non-military boundary policed by military patrols, a demarcation as opposed to a defence. It is the southern boundary of the military zone".

Finally, there was the "military way", which replaced the Stanegate and in places over-rode the *vallum* and which served for transport of supplies to the forts and milecastles.

The remains of these features are indicated on the Ordnance Survey 1 Inch maps, and in greater detail on their excellent special map of Hadrian's Wall on the scale of two inches to the mile. For a comprehensive account of the Wall the walker should read *Hadrian's Wall,* by A. R. Birley, published by H.M. Stationery Office, and *Handbook to the Roman Wall,* by J. Collingwood Bruce, edited by Ian A. Richmond and published by Andrew Reid, Newcastle upon Tyne.

The path which descends from the Carlisle road crosses the Stanegate and then runs alongside the *vallum* to the Greenhead-Gilsland road where a short length of the Wall is visible on the roadside.

From Thirlwall Castle, the remains of a fourteenth-century pele, built with stones from the Wall, we begin the traverse of the notched skyline of the Nine Nicks of Thirlwall. Two of the Nicks have been widened into ugly gashes by the quarrying of the Whin Sill.

For the next nine miles the Way follows the line of the Wall, passing the remains of the fort of *Aesica,* which had a six-mile-long aqueduct bringing water from the Caw Burn; climbing to Winshields, the highest point of the Wall (1,230 ft.) which commands views from Cross Fell and Skiddaw to the hills beyond Solway Firth; and continuing along the top of the crags overlooking Crag Lough and on by Hotbank Crags and Cuddy's Crags, the popular viewpoint for photographers, to leave the Wall at Rapishaw Gap. The Roman fort at Housesteads is a mile farther on, but should be visited. Shortly before reaching Housesteads we come to milecastle 37. The springers of the arch of the north gate still remain and the jambs are out of perpendicular, the result of the revolt in A.D. 197 and an attempt to destroy the milecastle.

Housesteads, possibly known to the Romans as *Vercovicium*, is the most impressive of the Wall forts. Approached from the west, a path leads down to a small museum worthy of a visit, where maps, models and plans give a clear idea of the fort as it appeared in the third and fourth centuries when it housed the one-thousand-strong First Cohort of Tungrians, so named as coming from around Tongres in Belgium.

Inside the fort, notice boards help one to find the four massive gateways with stones grooved by chariot wheels, the headquarters building, the commandant's house, the barracks and the granaries. These are described in detail in the official guide to Housesteads, published by H.M. Stationery Office.

Outside the fort was a civil settlement including shops and taverns. One of these is named the "Murder House"— the remains of a man and woman of the early fourth century having been buried under the floor, the

The Cheviots, looking west from Lamb Hill

man still having the point of a knife in his ribs.

South of the fort was an underground temple for the worship of Mithras, the Persian sun-god; hence Kipling's "Mithras, God of the Morning, our trumpets waken the Wall".

From Housesteads we retrace our steps for a mile to rejoin the Pennine Way at Rapishaw Gap between Cuddy's Crags and Hotbank Crags. Thence it runs between Greenlee and Broomlee Loughs near to Stonefolds, through a Forestry Commission plantation, and then over Hawk Side to enter another plantation by Kimmins Cross. Here, according to legend, Cumming, a northern chieftain, was slain by sons of King Arthur who then lived at Sewingshields Castle east of Housesteads.

Through the plantation a track leads to Ladyhill. Then the Way continues, crosses the Warks Burn, and goes on by Ash and Leadgate, and then over the Houxty Burn. By Shitlington Crags it rises to Ealingham Rigg and descends by Fell End to B6320, a mile and a half short of Bellingham on the North Tyne.

Bellingham (local pronunciation Bellingjam) is a

dour-looking, straggling village with a wide and windy street. The Early Norman church of St. Cuthbert is roofed with heavy stone flags carried on hexagonal stone ribs. Twice the chancel was burned by raiding Scots, and the narrow windows in the massive walls could have been designed for defence.

The Pennine Way does not pass by Hareshaw Linn where the stream plunges nearly 100 feet over a sandstone outcrop, because a right of way was not available above the fall. Instead it runs by the youth hostel and Blakelaw and Hareshaw House. If staying the night in Bellingham, the Linn can be visited on an evening stroll.

Over the heights of Lough Shaw and Lord's Shaw the Way continues through the parish of Troughend, a reminder of one of the most sanguinary of the Border ballads. It tells how Parcy Reed of Troughend Hall had to the hunting gone with three false Halls of Girstonfield. They stole the bridle of his steed, put water in his long gun and fixed his sword within its sheath. They then deserted him as his enemies approached. These were five men, named Crozier, from Liddesdale. The ballad tells that:

> "They fell upon him all at once,
> They mangled him most cruellie;
> The slightest wound might cause his deid,
> And they hae gi'en him thirty-three.
> They hacked off his hands and feet,
> And left him lying on the lee."

Three miles to the east is the village of Otterburn where in 1388 Earl Douglas and Sir Henry Percy (Hotspur) led their men into battle and

> "Earl Douglas was buried at the bracken bush
> And the Percy led captive away."

A boundary fence marks the Way over South and North Padon and over Brownrigg Head. The monument on Padon Hill commemorates Alexander Peden, one of the Scottish Covenanters, who used to meet in secluded places in the neighbourhood.

From the heights the Way descends through a forestry plantation to Blakehopeburnhaugh on the banks of the Rede.

Windy Gyle

Out of Redesdale we climb Byrness Hill, and then on over Ravens Knowe and Ogre Hill whence we look down on the rectangular outlines of the Roman camps at Chew Green. These are on Dere Street, Agricola's road from York to Scotland.

To reach the camps we cross a tiny trickle, the head-stream of the River Coquet, which has cut a valley of deep, swinging curves through the Cheviots.

Between Chew Green and Cheviot the line of the Pennine Way is marked by cairns erected by Tyneside ramblers. Dere Street is followed for half a mile to the Border Fence where, a few yards beyond a wicket gate, there is the outline of a Roman signal station.

For the next twelve miles we follow a high-level route by Lamb Hill and Beefstand Hill, by Mozie Law and Windy Gyle and Cairn Hill to Muckle Cheviot.[1] The hills have been grazed by sheep for centuries though there are stretches of heather and bilberry, and wet places where cotton-grass and sphagnum grow. On either hand are great swelling hills. The hump of

Cheviot overtops its neighbours from the Schil round to Hedgehope, Bloodybush Edge and Cushat Law. South-easterly, the sharp-featured Simonside Hills are prominent. Farther away the level brow of Cross Fell may be discerned, with Skiddaw and the Lake District hills faint in the distance.

On the Scottish side the triple peaks of the Eildon Hills are distinctive, but the view ranges from the Lammermuirs in the north-east to the Ettrick Hills in the north-west.

On Windy Gyle (2,034 ft.) there is a large mound of stones which the map names Russell's Cairn. It is said to commemorate a Lord Russell, slain in July 1585 at a meeting of the Wardens of the Marches. These meetings were held to hear claims and settle disputes but on this occasion a quarrel arose, Lord Russell went to investigate and was shot down.

In his book *The Border Line,* J. Logan Mack says another cairn half a mile to the north-east was formerly known as Russell's Cairn. Both cairns, he thinks, are Bronze Age burial mounds.

A mile and a half beyond Windy Gyle the Way crosses Clennell Street, a grass-grown track coming out of Coquetdale and descending the valley of Bowmont Water.

Cheviot is a wide featureless plateau with some peat groughs, though they are not so deep or intricate as those on Kinder Scout. As is usual with such broad heights, the best views are from the edges rather than the centre. East of the summit pole there is a pile of stones with recesses providing shelter from winds from any quarter.

The Pennine Way doubles back from Cheviot to Cairn Hill and then follows the Border Fence over Auchope Cairn, where there are several tall, pillar-like cairns, and on round the head of the College Burn valley on to the Schil (1,985 ft.). This conical height, with its coxcomb crest of rocks, is a good viewpoint, with Cheviot and the gorge of the Hen Hole on one hand, and on the other the long range of heights we have followed from Brownhart Law above the Chew

The end of the Pennine Way. The village green
at Kirk Yetholm

Green camps to Cheviot.

In the col between the Schil and Black Hag, where a
path comes up by the Fleehope Burn out of the College
Valley, we go through a gate in a wall and step into
Scotland, to follow the contour on the east side of
Latchly Hill and descend the Halterburn Valley to
Kirk Yetholm.

This unpretentious Border village was for centuries
a gipsy settlement and a very modest cottage is still
known as Gipsy Palace.

Jean Gordon of Kirk Yetholm was, Sir Walter Scott
says, the gipsy on whom the character of Meg Merrilees
was founded. In *Guy Mannering* Meg is described as
six feet high, and Keats wrote:

> "Old Meg was brave as Margaret Queen,
> And tall as an Amazon.
> An old red blanket cloak she wore,
> A chip hat had she on.
> God rest her aged bones somewhere—
> She died full long agone."

Here, 250 miles from our starting point, you may agree with C. E. Montague that "the Pennine has done its big things. The way that its strata are bent and worn has shaped the industrial history of England. A kind of life that is not precisely lived anywhere else made the Brontës just what they were. On Pennine heights there stick out the raw ends of forces that help to set us all our work and to map out our lives."

Falcon

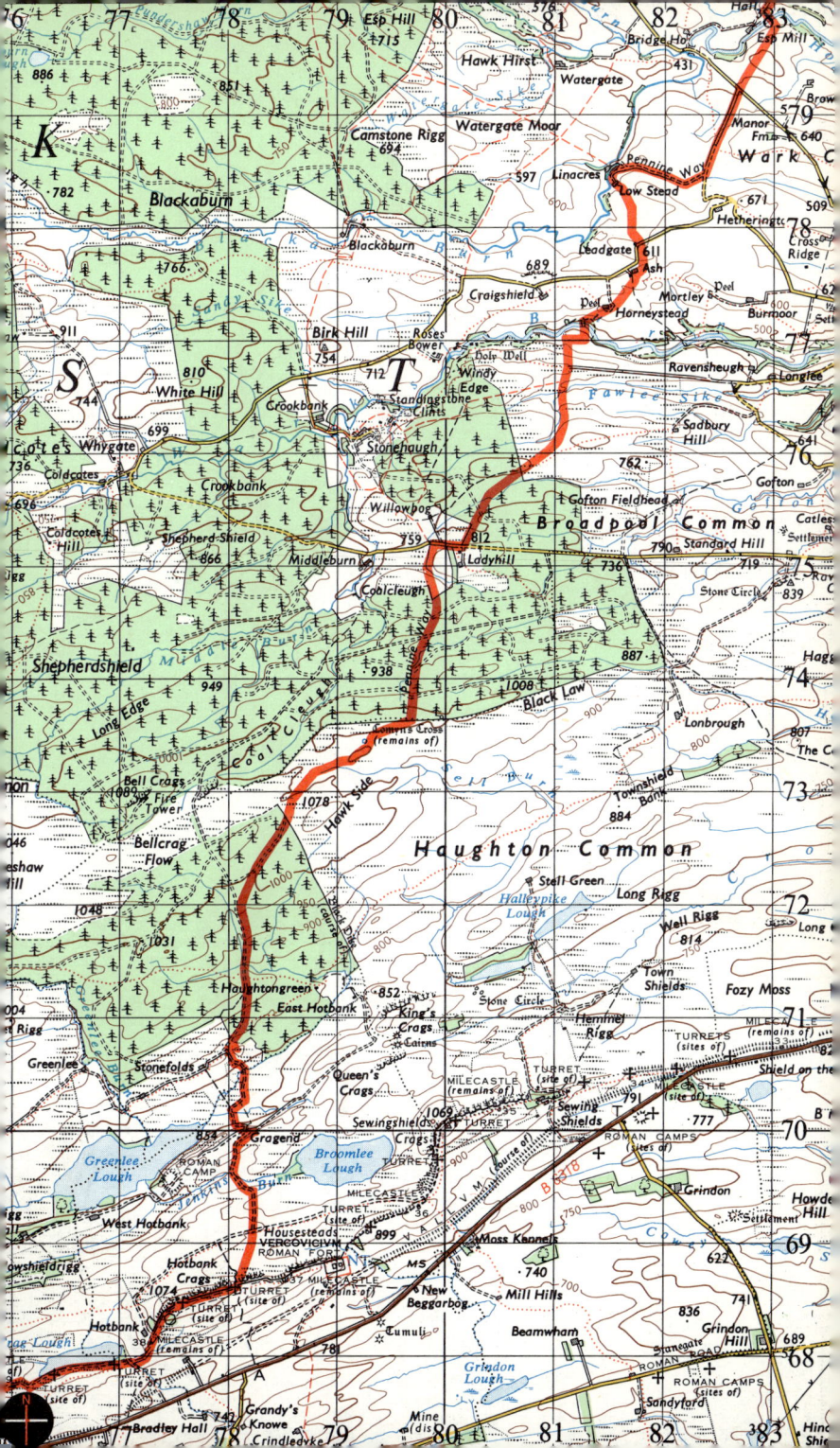

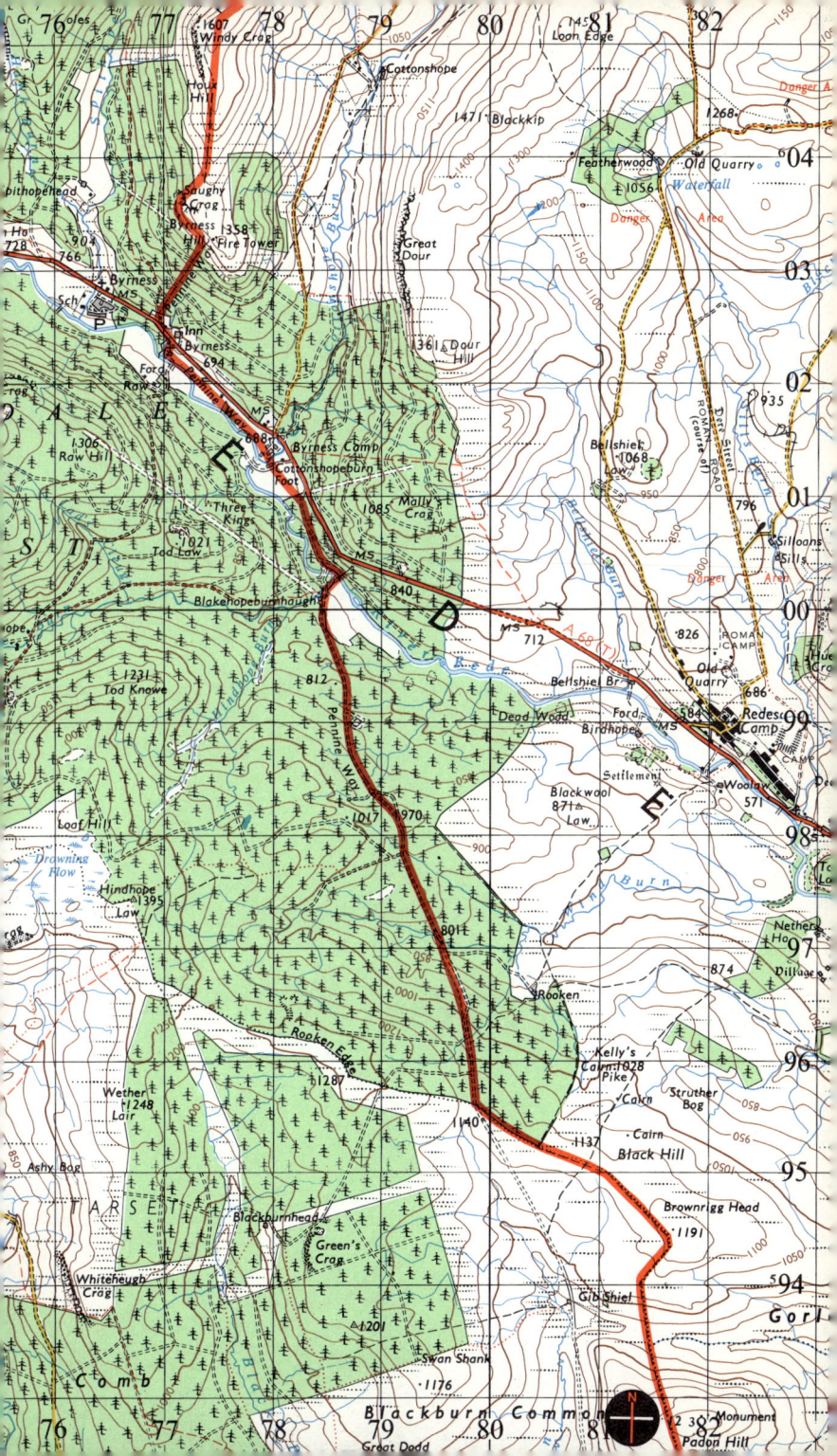

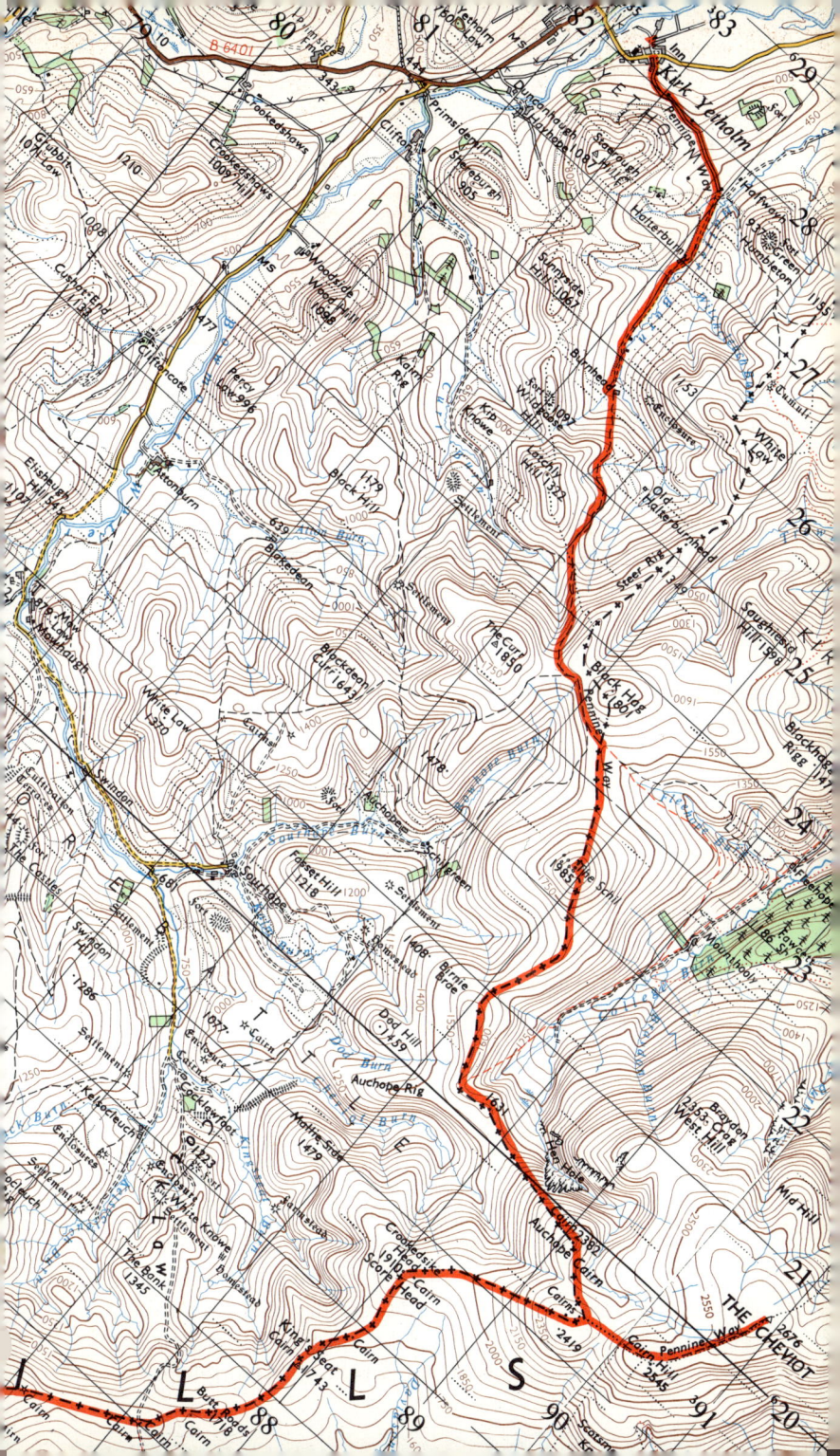

CHAPTER SEVEN

Hints by the Way

For a normally healthy person properly shod, clothed according to the weather and capable of steering a course by map and compass, the Pennine Way presents no great hazards except occasionally in wintry weather. Then it may prove more difficult and more exhausting than hill walking in the Lake District or North Wales. The weather is often more severe than in those areas. The tops are more extensive than mountains like Scafell Pike, Snowdon or Tryfan. Heather, peat, bog and tussocks of rough grass, too, are more tiring than the well-trodden tracks on those mountains.

Even in summer there are cold and wet days, though they may not deter a reasonably fit walker. He may enjoy battling against wind and rain and relying on his compass to keep a course across cloud-draped Kinder Scout or Cross Fell. Even a seasoned fell-walker may admit, though, that the best part of such a day is the relaxation in a healthy glow after a bath, a change into dry clothes and a good meal. There are, however, times when conditions may prove, as they have on a number of occasions, beyond the endurance of tough and experienced walkers.

Dress and Equipment

A few hints on dress and equipment may be useful for those unaccustomed to this kind of walking. Boots are preferable to shoes for the saving of strain on the ankles. They are more likely to keep the feet dry and also to keep out grit, small pebbles and bits of heather which can soon set up abrasions. The boots should be lightly nailed in soles and heels to give a bite on steep grass slopes. *Vibram* type rubber soles are now more popular than nails, but they become clogged with soft peat or mud and do not give the same grip on grass or wet boulders. Woollen socks or stockings should be worn—two pairs if the boots will take them.

To cope with wide ranges of temperature a windproof and possibly shower-proof jacket coming below the waist is useful with a spare pullover handy to slip on when resting in a cooling breeze.

A lightweight, loosely fitting waterproof coat or cape will give some protection against rain, but don't expect to find a perfect, waterproof garment.

A rucksack affords the easiest way of carrying your necessities, but remember the advice of a veteran hill-walker: first pack your rucksack; then empty it on the floor and repack, leaving at home half the things you first thought of.

There are signposts where the Way crosses roads in the valleys, and on the hills much of the route is marked with cairns. For further guidance the Countryside Commission have placed display boards at the points listed on page 106 with the local section of the Way marked on Ordnance Survey $2\frac{1}{2}$ Inches to 1 Mile maps.

A compass is essential equipment at all times, especially when the clouds come down and visibility is reduced to a few yards. When that seems likely, keep an eye on the weather and carefully note your progress so that you know your position on the map when all landmarks are hidden. So, too, if the weather worsens you can, with the aid of the map, decide on the quickest and safest descent.

If there is a stiff breeze blowing there are likely to be occasional breaks in the cloud sometimes, giving an opportunity to recognise features in the landscape.

Notes on Difficult Sections

The following notes may help less-experienced walkers in negotiating some of the more difficult parts of the Way.

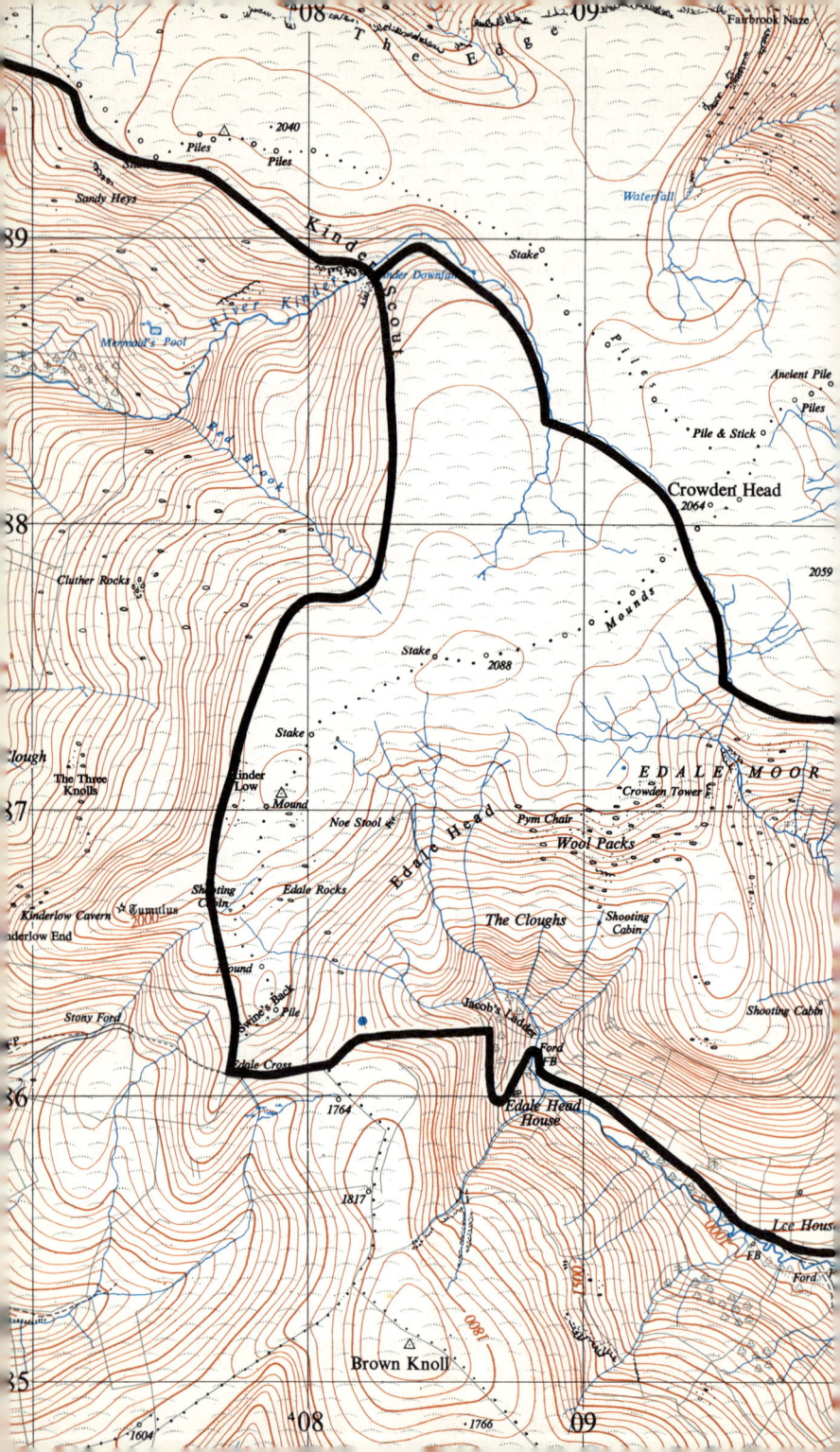

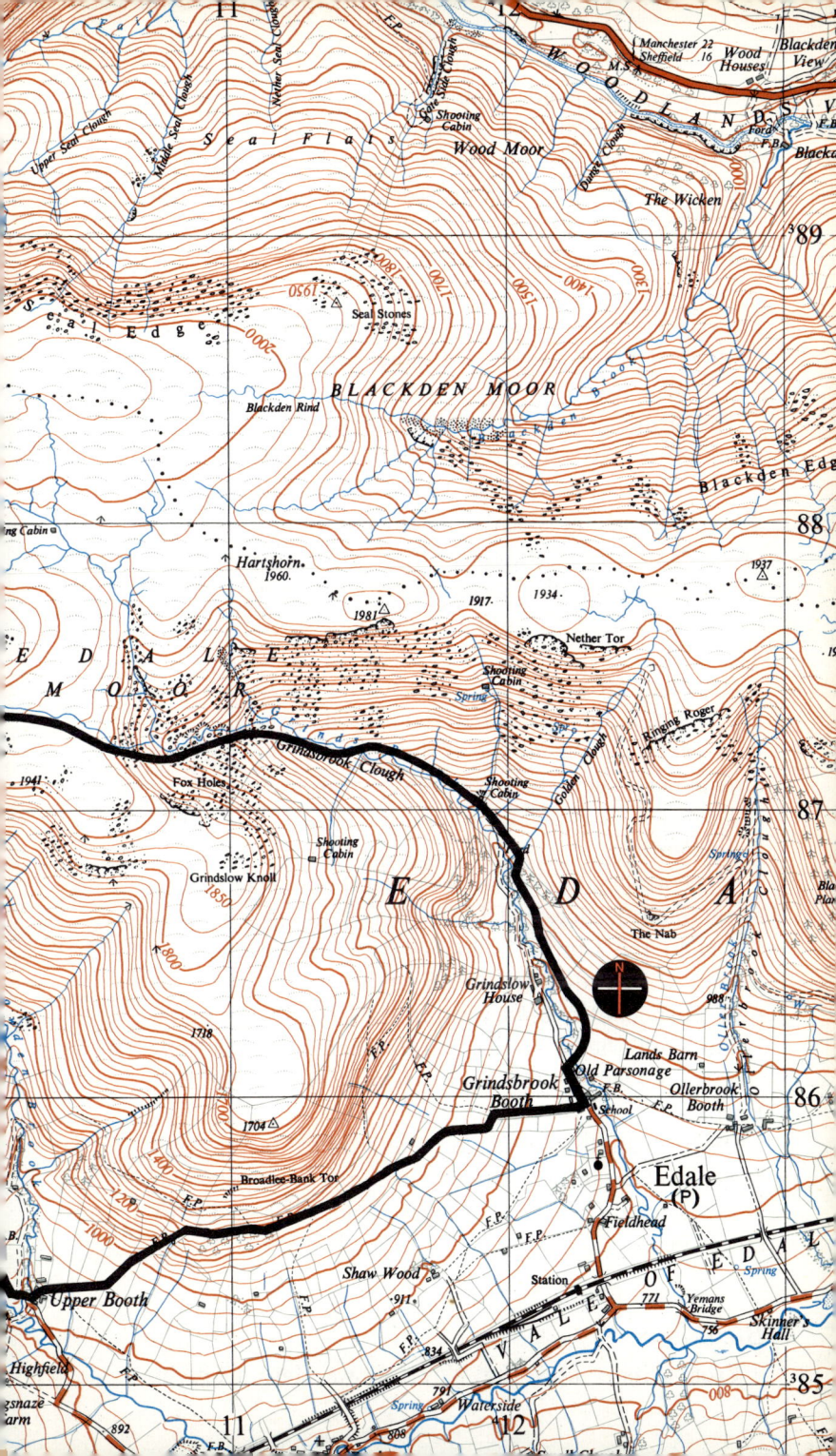

Kinder Scout

The maps on pages 88 and 89 and the Peak District tourist map, published by Ordnance Survey, show the alternative Pennine Way route from Edale by Broadlee Bank and Upper Booth to Edale Cross and thence northerly near the Ordnance Survey trigonometrical point on Kinder Low, and then roughly along the western edge of the Moor to Kinder Downfall. This is intended as a bad-weather route and it avoids the boggy section between the head-streams of Crowden Brook and Kinder River.

The ordinary route follows the Grinds Brook until it forks. A steep ascent of the left branch leads to the edge of the plateau. The Way then runs westward, first along a series of groughs which eventually fade out, then crossing several groughs draining southwards, keeping a few yards south of some strangely weathered boulders and so reaching Crowden Brook north of Crowden Tower.

Crowden Brook is followed northwards, avoiding several branches on the left and one on the right, until it peters out in the middle of the plateau. Here there is a tendency to deviate eastwards towards the slight rise of Crowden Head and even into the head of the Grindsbrook Valley.

The correct route is north-west across the bog to one of the main feeders of Kinder River which is then followed to the Downfall. In bad weather the western branch of Crowden Brook can be followed until it dies out. Then continue westwards crossing the groughs leading into the River Noe and so reaching the alternative route south of the point where it crosses the Red Brook.

If unfortunate enough to be on Kinder in the dark remember that in a number of places, particularly at the Downfall and Crowden Tower, the moor is edged with steep rocks.

Bleaklow

From Alport Low the Way follows Hern Clough,

crossing a series of deep groughs which are easier to negotiate on the west side of the main channel. In mist the only indication of the summit is a stretch of easier walking free from groughs and over a mixture of sand and peat sprinkled with quartz pebbles.

From the summit of Bleaklow a course about 20 degrees west of north should be followed—a few degrees farther west will not matter. This will lead into the area drained by two converging streams leading into Torside Clough. Either of these may be safely followed to their confluence. There, John Track Well may be seen on the western stream. The Way mounts the opposite bank and runs for a third of a mile roughly parallel with the Torside stream, keeping east of Torside Castle (not west as shown on some Ordnance Survey maps). Next the route is along Clough Edge, with deepening Torside Clough on the right and then descending to a track west of Reaps Farm. Bleaklow is a wide expanse of moor and bog and the greatest care should be taken to avoid straying eastwards. If in doubt descend south-west to Doctor's Gate and Shelf Brook or west to the Glossop-Woodhead road, B6105.

Black Hill

The top of Black Hill is indeed black: a flat expanse of powdery and often squelchy peat. From that top to the road A635 and then by White Moss and Black Moss, is a difficult section best avoided in bad weather in favour of the following alternative:

The summit is marked by an Ordnance Survey trigonometrical point and this should be located by traverses in various directions before losing any height. Once it is found, walk north-east and so reach one or other of the feeders of Hey Clough into which you descend. Keep on the left of the main stream and left of a waterfall. Look for a short length of wall on the opposite side of the stream. From that point a boundary ditch leads in a straight line north-west to the road A635 at Wessenden Head. Cross the road A635, continue north-east to

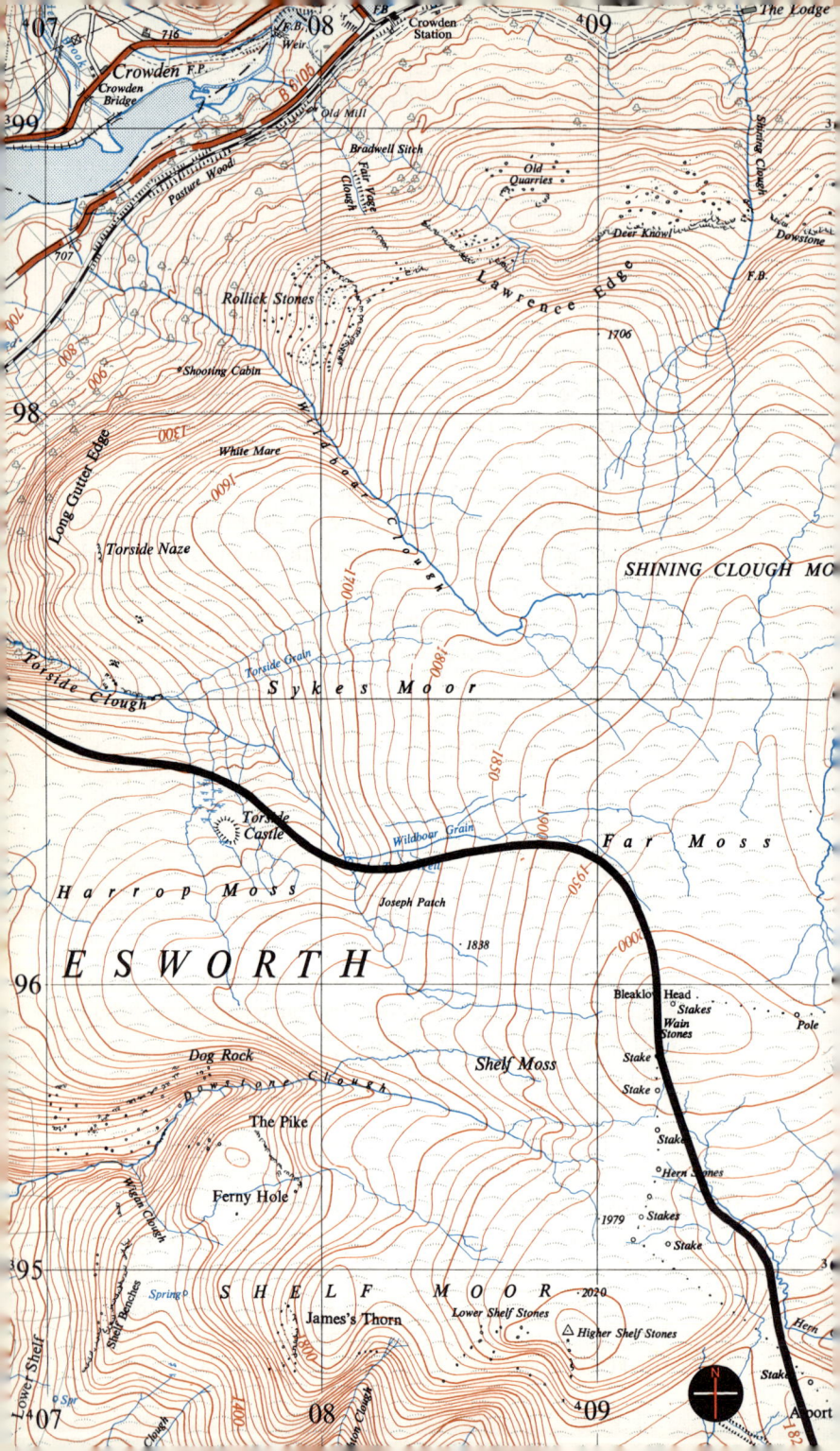

the Meltham Road and then turn left on the path down Wessenden Valley.

Below Wessenden Reservoir cross the brook and mount by Blakeley Clough (not named on O.S. 1 Inch map) round the north side of Black Moss to the southern corner of the more westerly of the two reservoirs and thence to Standedge.

To reach Longdendale from Black Hill in bad weather, take a course south-west from the summit, but don't be misled by some streamlets which are reached about 250 yards from the Ordnance Survey obelisk. These run south-west for another 500 yards and then swing north. At that point keep walking south-west to the beginnings of Crowden Great Brook. The stream can be followed without danger, passing below Laddow Rocks, as far as Oaken Clough. Two hundred yards up that Clough there is a well-trodden track, on which turn left for Crowden.

Great Shunner Fell

East of the summit cairn a wire fence provides an easy escape route. In places the wires may have disappeared but the posts remain and indicate a line which can be followed to the Buttertubs Pass road.

Birkdale to High Cup Nick

This length of a little more than four miles shows no obvious difficulties on the map, but there are many records of walkers going astray. Some of them seem to have crossed Maize Beck too far downstream and then followed a track by Swarth Gill and down Hilton Gill.

Three hundred yards south-west of the upper farm at Birkdale the Pennine Way crosses Grain Beck, then ascends to the mine dumps at Moss Shop. The route is cairned from there to a ford on Maize Beck. From there the official route is upstream on the north bank of the river as far as a footbridge.

If the river is fordable, easier walking will be found on the old bridleway on the south side of the river. This length is cairned to the head of High Cup Gill.

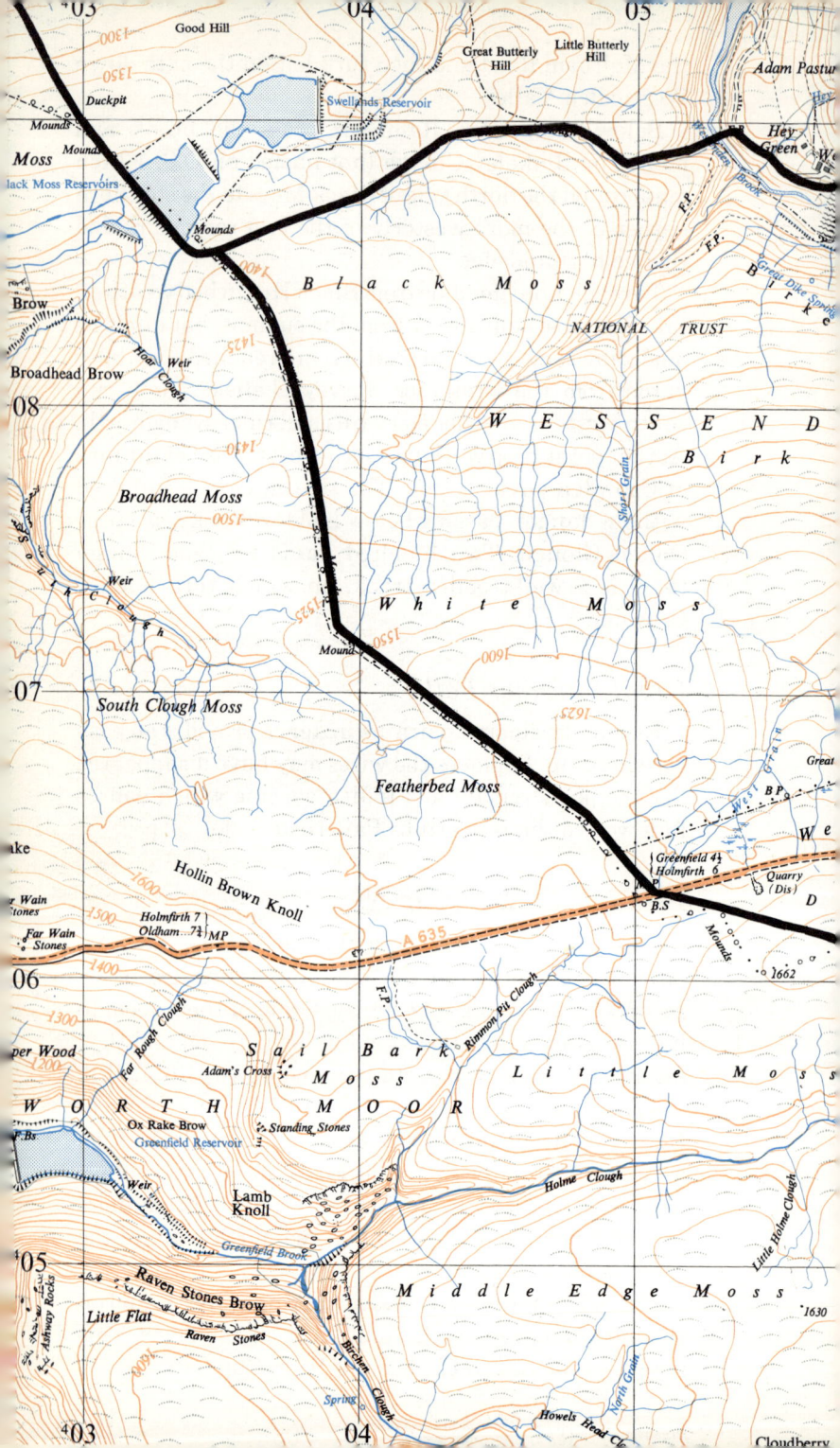

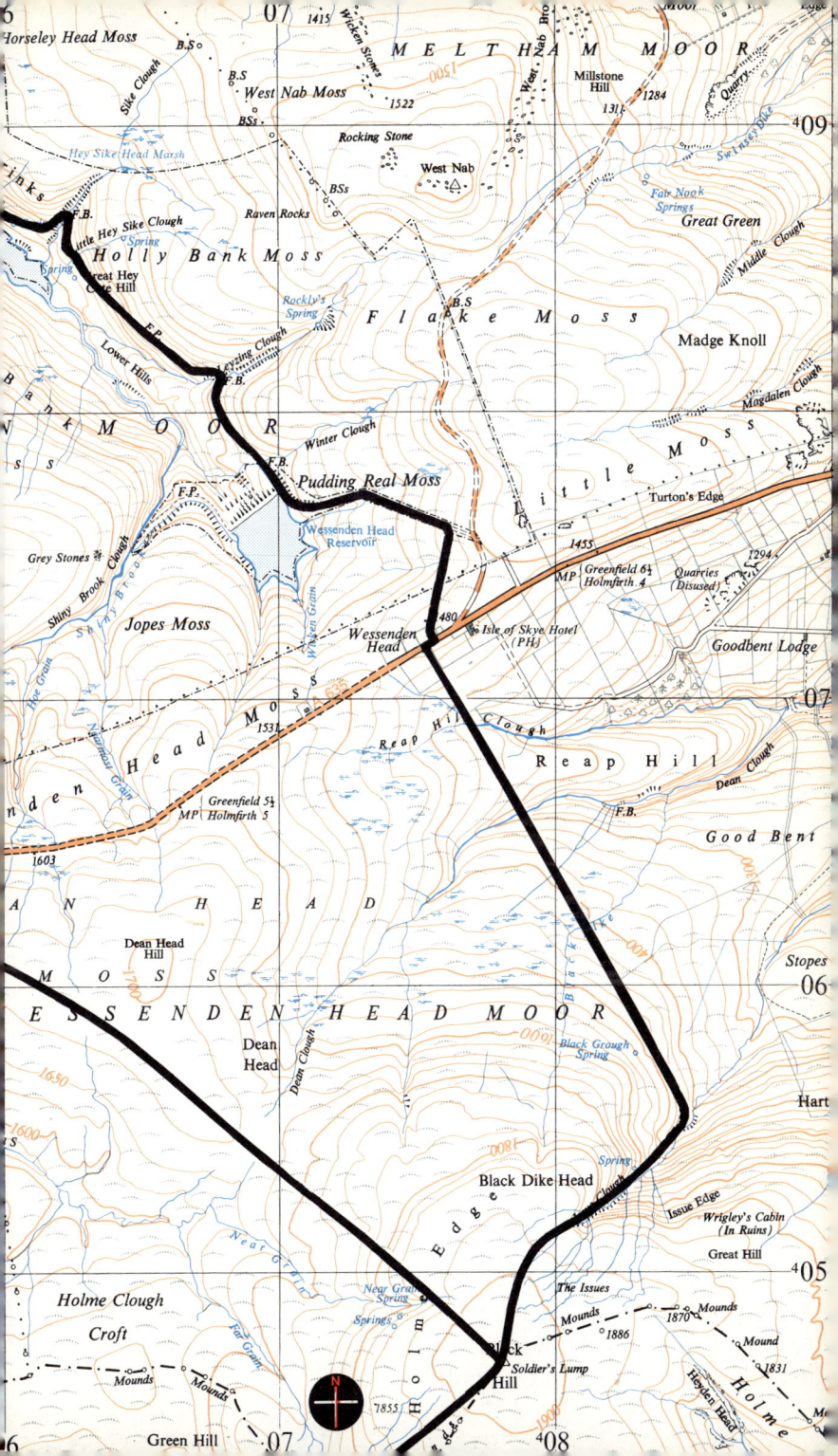

If the northern route has been followed, a south-westerly course from the bridge will lead across a grassy flat to the head of the Gill. From there a cairned track runs on the north-west side of the Gill down to a sheep-fold, beyond which there is an obvious track down to Town Head on the edge of Dufton village.

Cross Fell

This, the highest hill in the Pennines, is a plateau a mile across from east to west and half a mile from south to north. To the east there is an extensive, boggy waste drained by the Tees. By all means avoid straying into this desolate area.

The Pennine Way descends Little Dun Fell to a wet depression drained by Crowdundle Beck to the west, and to the east by the Tees, both streams hereabouts being little more than trickles. A fence crossing this watershed marks the Cumberland-Westmorland boundary. Beyond the fence, Crowdundle Beck can be followed upstream until a line of cairns is reached. These lead up through a ring of boulders fringing the summit plateau. Once above these a north-north-west course will lead to the huge summit cairn. A few yards due north of this there is a small cairn giving the line across the plateau. If that line is maintained a large cairn will be reached on the northern edge of the plateau marking the way down to the Kirkland-Garrigill track which can be followed without difficulty.

If visibility is very limited and you fail to locate the summit cairn, walk westwards to the edge of the plateau, then follow it round towards the north. There are some cairns on this western edge which can be ignored. Keep a check on your compass until you find you are walking east and then watch for a large cairn. Descend a few yards below it and cast about for Crossfell Well. To the west of the Well there is a rough stone enclosure (with the flat slab mentioned on page 61). A descent north-north-west from here will lead to the Kirkland-Garrigill track. You are now back on the Pennine Way. Turn right, passing the workings of old lead mines on the seven miles walk to Garrigill.

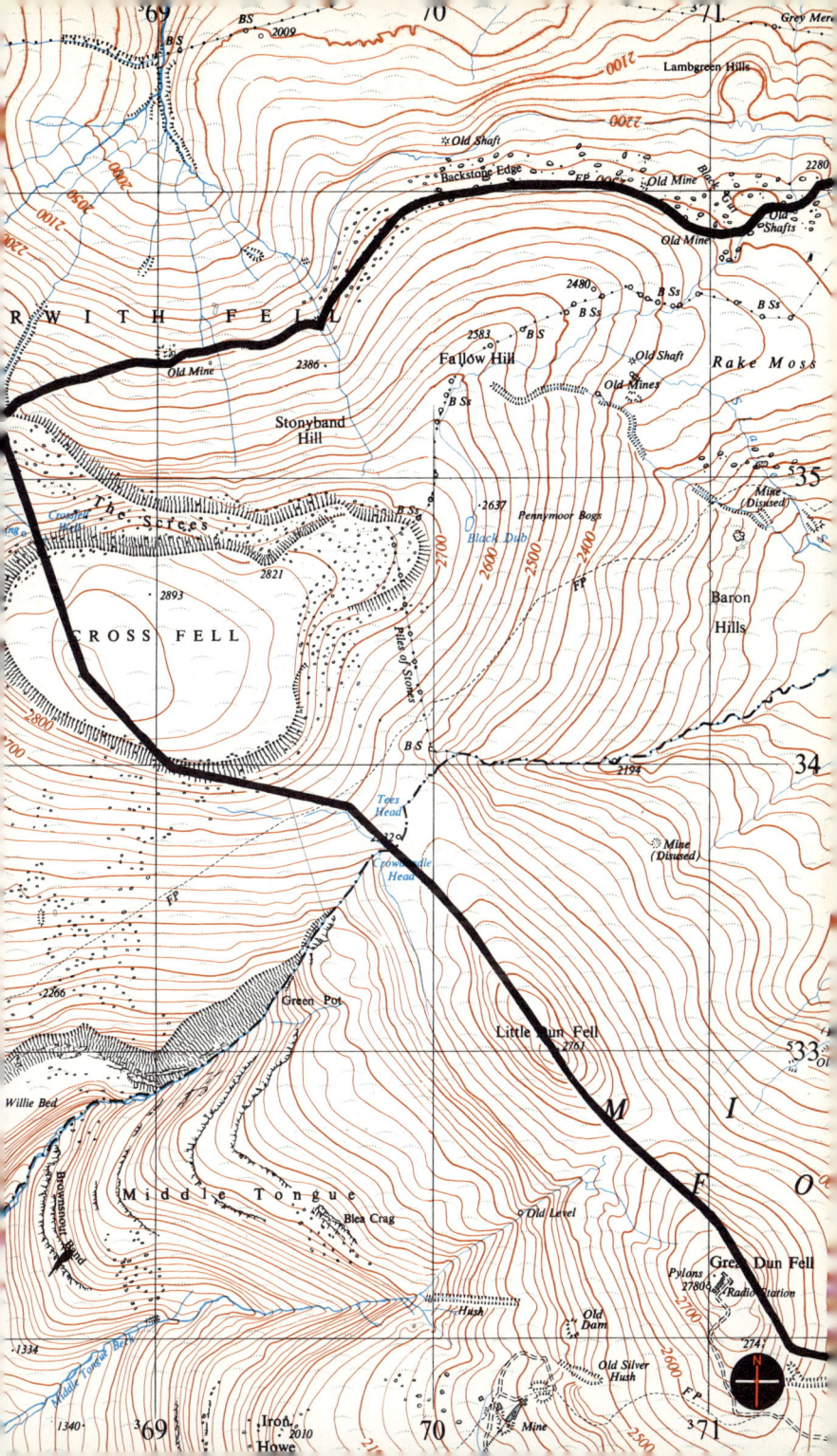

When bad weather is met in the Cheviots, the dearth of accommodation must be kept in mind. Between Chew Green and Windy Gyle, escape should be sought by descending southerly to the valley of the Coquet. Many paths and bridleways suitable for this are shown on the map, but not all of them are discernible on the ground.

From Chew Green the Coquet is a guiding line as far as Makendon, the first shepherd's cottage in the valley. Thence a road descends by Fulhope to Blindburn and down dale to Alwinton.

North and north-east of Chew Green, if you fail to find one of the ill-defined paths, you may safely follow one of the streams such as Buckham's Walls Burn, Blind Burn or Carlcroft Burn, down to the road.

Half a mile east of Mozie Law, there is a gate in a right-angled bend of the Border fence where an old track shown on the map as "The Street" comes up from Hownam on the Scottish side. This track is easy to follow southwards over Black Braes on to Hindside Knowe and down to the road at the confluence of the Rowhope Burn and the Coquet.

A mile north-east of Windy Gyle there is another well-defined track, Clennell Street. This may be followed on the Scottish side down to Cocklawfoot and down the valley of the Bowmont Water to Yetholm ten miles away.

On the English side Clennell Street leads down to the farm road below Uswayford. That road may be followed down the valley to Trows and Rowhope. Alternatively you may continue on Clennell Street, crossing the Usway Burn and descending by Wholehope to Alwinton.

Cheviot is another wide featureless top. Between the summit and Cairn Hill to the south there is a series of peat groughs draining westerly into the gorge of the Hen Hole. These, if followed upwards north-easterly, will bring you near the summit pole. A little east of this there is a large pile of stones with several recesses affording shelter from the wind.

The best escape route from anywhere on the summit

plateau is to descend due east to the Harthope Burn and
follow it downstream to Langleeford. From there it is
seven miles by road to Wooler.

Raven

CHAPTER EIGHT

Accommodation

Along the greater part of the route accommodation will be found in inns, farmhouses and cottages. In some of the larger villages there may be a choice of two or more addresses. Much as one may dislike walking to a fixed timetable, accommodation should be reserved in advance in Upper Teesdale, Dufton, Redesdale and Upper Coquetdale. Elsewhere, where a telephone number is given, it may be advisable before starting out in the morning to telephone to book accommodation for the evening.

There is a number of youth hostels on or near the route. These are listed at the end of this chapter. With the exception of the Crowden hostel, these are open only to members of the Youth Hostels Association who should consult their current handbook and check times of opening.

From Crowden to Blackstone Edge is a distance of 15 rough moorland miles. Anyone unwilling to face the next 8 miles over Stoodley Pike and across the Calder Valley to Colden might take the bus to Littleborough or Rochdale and return next morning to continue northwards.

Those not wishing to walk the 22 miles from Keld to Middleton in Teesdale should take the loop route to Bowes. This leaves the main route at Trough Heads and runs by East Mellwaters, Lady Mires and Swinholme, making twelve miles from Keld. From Bowes proceed by Tute Hill, Levy Pool and on the south and west sides of Goldsborough (1,274 ft.) to East Friar House and then west to rejoin the main route at Blackton Bridge.

Anyone who has spent the night at Spithopehead may follow the track to Greyhound Law and round the Hearts Toe to join the Pennine Way a little north of the Coquet.

For Carlcroft in Upper Coquetdale there is a path (not very distinct) along the southern slopes of Lamb Hill, crossing the Blind Burn and descending Carlcroft Hill. Easier to follow is the track, known as "The Street", over Black Braes on to Hindside Knowe and then descending right for Carlcroft or left for Rowhope and Trows—the only houses providing accommodation between Redesdale and Yetholm.

Lapwing

Youth Hostels

Youth Hostels Association (England and Wales)

Headquarters: Trevelyan House, 8 St. Stephen's Hill, St. Albans, Herts.
Peak Regional Office[1]:
Secretary, 3 Leopold Street, Derby.
Yorkshire Regional Office[2]:
Secretary, 96 Main Street, Bingley, Yorkshire.
Border and Dales Regional Office[3]:
Honorary Secretary, 30 Baliol Square, Lowes Barn, Durham.
Lakeland Regional Office[4]:
Secretary, Church Street, Windermere, Westmorland.

Scottish Youth Hostels Association

Headquarters: 7 Glebe Crescent, Stirling.
Edinburgh District Office[5]:
Secretary, 7 Bruntsfield Crescent, Edinburgh 10.

Hostels on or near the Pennine Way

Edale[1]	(G.R.140866)	The Warden, The Youth Hostel, Rowland Cote, Nether Booth, Edale, Sheffield, Yorks.
Crowden[1]	(G.R.073994)	The Warden, Peak National Park Hostel, Crowden, Hadfield, Hyde, Cheshire.
Mankinholes[2]	(G.R.960235)	The Warden, The Youth Hostel, Mankinholes, Todmorden, Lancs.
Earby[2]	(G.R.915468)	The Warden, The Katherine Bruce Glasier Memorial Hostel, Birch Hall Lane, Earby, Colne, Lancs.
Malham[2]	(G.R.901629)	The Warden, The John Dower Memorial Hostel, Malham, Skipton, Yorks.
Stainforth[2]	(G.R.821668)	The Warden, Stainforth Youth Hostel, Settle, Yorks.
Hawes[2]	(G.R.868898)	The Warden, The Youth Hostel, Hawes, Yorks.

Crowden Hostel

Keld[3]	(G.R.892009)	The Warden, The Youth Hostel, Keld Lodge, Keld, Richmond, Yorks.
Langdon Beck[3]	(G.R.860304)	The Warden, Langdon Beck Youth Hostel, Forest in Teesdale, Barnard Castle, Co. Durham.
Knock[4]	(G.R.680279)	The Warden, The Youth Hostel, Knock, Appleby, Westmorland.
Once Brewed[3]	(G.R.752668)	The Warden, Once Brewed Youth Hostel, Military Road, Bardon Mill, Hexham, Northumberland.
Bellingham[3]	(G.R.843834)	The Warden, The Youth Hostel, Woodburn Road, Bellingham, Hexham, Noıthumberland.
Byrness[3]	(G.R.764028)	The Warden, The Youth Hostel, 7 Otterburn Green, Byrness, Newcastle upon Tyne.
Kirk Yetholm[5]	(G.R.826282)	The Warden, The Youth Hostel, Kelso, Roxburghshire.

Meadow pipit

National Park Information Centres

Northumberland

Byrness: 9 Otterburn Green, Byrness, Otterburn
                    (Tel. Otterburn 622).

Ingram: The Old School House (Tel. Powburn 248).

Once Brewed: Military Road, Bardon Mill, Hexham
                    (Tel. Bardon Mill 396). Mobile.

Peak District

Bakewell: The Market Hall, Bridge Street
                    (Tel. Bakewell 3227).

Buxton: St Ann's Well, The Crescent (Tel. 2060).

Castleton: Castle Street (Tel. Hope 679).

Edale: Field Head (Tel. Edale 207). Mobile.

Yorkshire Dales (North Riding)

Aysgarth Falls: Leyburn, Yorks. (Tel. 424).

Yorkshire Dales (West Riding)

Clapham (via Lancaster): Reading Room (Tel. 419).

Malham (caravan):   The Car Park.

A Pennine Way walker traces his route on the mapboard at
Gargrave

The Pennine Way

7

The Pennine Way is one of the long-distance footpaths planned by the Countryside Commission. It enables walkers to follow the Pennine Chain from Edale in the Peak District National Park to the Scottish Border – a journey of about 250 miles across predominantly wild hill country.

On the high moorlands the going is rough and strenuous, and can be dangerous in bad weather. Here proper equipment is needed – strong boots, protective clothing, map and compass.

The map below shows the local section of the Pennine Way on a scale of two and a half inches to one mile (1:25.000).

Official guidebook, The Pennine Way by Tom Stephenson, with Ordnance Survey maps in colour, photographs and drawings. Published by H.M. Stationery Office.

The Country Code

Help to preserve the beauty of the countryside, and avoid damaging farm property, stock and crops by following rules of the Country Code.

Leave no litter – take it home

Guard against all risks of fire

Fasten all gates

Keep dogs under proper control

Keep to the paths across farmland

Avoid damaging fences, hedges and walls

Safeguard water supplies

Protect wild life, wild plants and trees

Go carefully on country roads

Respect the life of the countryside

Location of Pennine Way Display Boards

		O.S. Grid Reference
1	Edale	122861
2	Crowden	073994
3	Saddleworth (A62)	015093
4	Blackstone Edge	969179
5	Old Snap/Dean Fields	987375
6	Lothersdale	959459
7	Gargrave	932541
8	Malham	901628
9	Horton in Ribblesdale	808726
10	Hawes	871898
11	Thwaite	892982
12	Bowes	996135
13	Middleton in Teesdale	984254
14	Widdybank Farm	837298
15	Dufton	689251
16	Garrigill	745415
17	Slaggyford	678525
18	Greenhead	649651
19	Steel Rigg (Hadrian's Wall)	751677
20	Bellingham	839834
21	Lord's Shaw	824917
22	Byrness	771023
23	Windy Gyle	871160
24	Kirk Yetholm	826282

The Country Code

Guard Against All Risk of Fire

Every year costly damage is done by fire to crops, plantations, woodlands and heaths. Picnic fires not properly put out are one cause. A cigarette thrown away or a pipe carelessly knocked out can start a raging inferno. Be careful—a spark may do terrible damage and destroy a lifetime's work.

Fasten All Gates

Animals, if they stray, can do great damage to crops and to themselves too. Wandering animals are a menace to themselves and to others on country roads. Even if you find a gate open, always shut it after you.

Keep Dogs Under Proper Control

It is natural for a dog to chase anything that will run. Keep yours out of temptation's way. Animals are easily frightened. The chasing of a ewe or cow may mean the loss of valuable young. Town-bred dogs run great risks from traffic in narrow roads. When near animals or walking along the road, keep your dog on the lead, if it cannot be kept under close control.

Keep to the Paths Across Farm Land

Crops are damaged by treading at any stage of growth. Patches of flattened corn in a field make it difficult to harvest. Grass also is a valuable crop, remember. So please walk in single file on field paths. This keeps the track well defined and saves the crop on either side.

Avoid Damaging Fences, Hedges and Walls

If you force your way through a fence or hedge, you will weaken it. Where a man has gone an animal may follow. Stones from walls rolled down slopes may injure people and animals, destroy fences, and damage crops or machines. Use gates and stiles.

Leave No Litter

All litter is unsightly. Broken glass, tins and plastic bags are dangerous; they very easily maim livestock. Tins, bottles and stones in fields damage costly machinery. This may hold up work which it is vital to finish while the weather lasts. So take your picnic remains and other litter home with you.

Safeguard Water Supplies

Water is precious in the country. Never wash dishes or bathe in somebody's water supply or foul it in any other way, or interfere with water-troughs set for cattle.

Protect Wild Life, Wild Plants and Trees

Wild flowers give more pleasure to more people if left to grow. Plants should never be uprooted. Trees are valuable as well as beautiful: if they are damaged their health and beauty is harmed. Birds and their eggs, animals, plants and trees should be left alone.

Go Carefully on Country Roads

Country roads have special dangers. Blind corners, hump-backed bridges, slow-moving farm machinery and led or driven animals are all hazards for the motorist. Walk carefully, too. It is generally safer to walk on the right, facing oncoming traffic.

Respect the Life of the Countryside

The life of the country centres on its work. While you are there, try to fit in. The countryman has to leave his belongings in the open; roads and paths run through his place of business, and the public are on trust. His work often involves hard labour. He has to keep early hours. So make as little noise as possible when you pass through his village in the evening. Be considerate, leave things alone, and so repay the local people for the pleasure their countryside has given you.

Bog asphodel (*Narthecium ossifragum*)

Bibliography

The Pennines and Adjacent Areas, W. Edwards and F. M. Trotter. 3rd Edition 1954. H.M.S.O.

Northern England, T. Eastwood. 3rd Edition 1953. H.M.S.O. (These are handbooks on regional geology.)

Geology of Yorkshire, P. F. Kendall and H. E. Wroot. 1924. Privately printed.

The Yorkshire Dales, C. A. M. King. 1960. Geographical Association.

An Account of the Mining Districts of Alston Moor, Weardale and Teesdale, T. Sopwith. 1833. W. Davison, Alnwick.

Two Centuries of Industrial Welfare, A. Raistrick. 1938. Friends' Historical Society.

Malham and Malham Moor, A. Raistrick. 1947. Dalesman Publishing Company.

Green Tracks on the Pennines, A. Raistrick. 1962. Dalesman Publishing Company.

The Face of North-West Yorkshire, A. Raistrick and J. Illingworth. 1949. Dalesman Publishing Company.

Mountains and Moorland, W. H. Pearsall. 1950. New Naturalists.

Mountain Flowers, J. Raven and M. Walters. 1956. New Naturalists.

Wild Flowers of Chalk and Limestone, J. E. Lousley. 1950. New Naturalists.

Climate and the British Scene, G. Manley. 1952. New Naturalists.

Britannia (Bishop Gibson's translation), W. Camden. 1722. London.

Concise Oxford Dictionary of English Placenames, E. Ekwall. 1936. O.U.P.

Roman Roads in Britain—Vol. 2, I. D. Margary. 1957. Phoenix.

Handbook to the Roman Wall (11th Edition edited by I. A. Richmond), J. Collingwood Bruce. 1957. Andrew Reid and Company, Newcastle upon Tyne.

Hadrian's Wall, A. R. Birley. 1963. H.M.S.O.

Housesteads Roman Fort, E. Birley. 1952. H.M.S.O.

History of Craven, T. D. Whitaker. 2nd Edition 1829. J. Dodgson, Leeds.

The Peak and the Pennines, W. A. Poucher. 1966. Constable.

West Yorkshire, J. W. Davis and F. A. Lees. 1878. L. Reeve and Company.

Craven and North-West Yorkshire, H. Speight. 1892. Elliot Stock.

Teesdale, D. M. Ramsden. 1947. Museum Press.

The Border Line, J. Logan Mack. 2nd Edition 1926. Oliver and Boyd.

Upper Coquetdale, D. D. Dixon. 1903. Redpath, Newcastle upon Tyne.

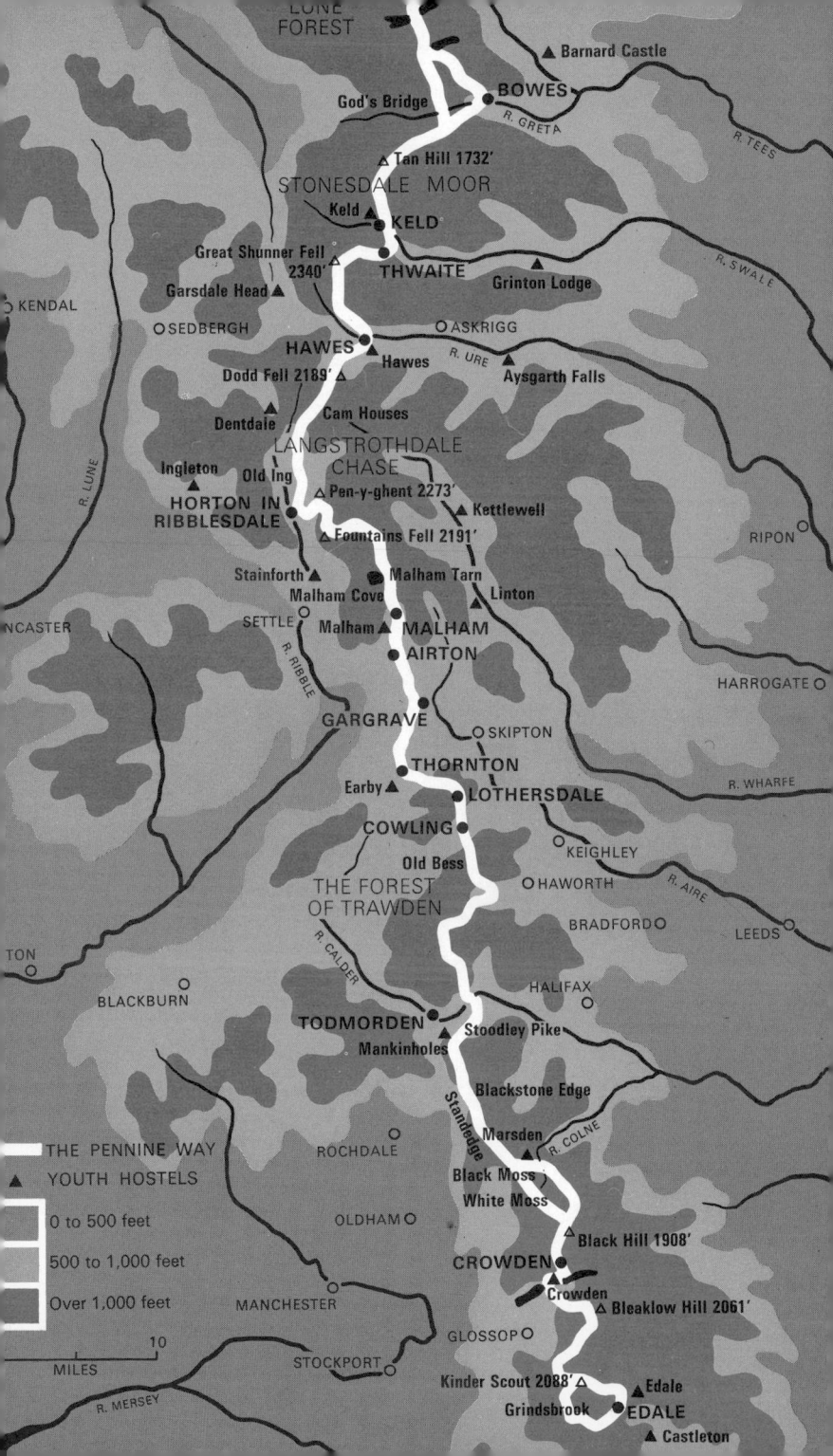

LUNE
FOREST

▲ Barnard Castle

God's Bridge

BOWES

R. GRETA

R. TEES

△ Tan Hill 1732'

STONESDALE MOOR

Keld ● KELD

Great Shunner Fell ▲
2340'

THWAITE

Grinton Lodge ▲

R. SWALE

Garsdale Head ▲

○ SEDBERGH

○ ASKRIGG

○ KENDAL

HAWES

Hawes ●

R. URE

Aysgarth Falls ▲

Dodd Fell 2189' △

Cam Houses ●

LANGSTROTHDALE
CHASE

Dentdale ●

Ingleton ▲

Old Ing ●

△ Pen-y-ghent 2273'

Kettlewell ▲

R. LUNE

HORTON IN
RIBBLESDALE ●

△ Fountains Fell 2191'

RIPON ○

Stainforth ● ▲

■ Malham Tarn

Malham Cove ●

Linton ●

SETTLE ○

Malham ▲ MALHAM

○ NCASTER

R. RIBBLE

AIRTON ●

HARROGATE ○

GARGRAVE ●

○ SKIPTON

THORNTON ●

R. WHARFE

Earby ● ▲

LOTHERSDALE ●

COWLING ●

○ KEIGHLEY

Old Bess ●

THE FOREST
OF TRAWDEN

○ HAWORTH

R. AIRE

BRADFORD ○

LEEDS ○

TON ○

R. CALDER

BLACKBURN ○

HALIFAX ○

TODMORDEN ● ▲ Stoodley Pike

Mankinholes ●

Blackstone Edge ●

Standedge

Marsden ●

R. COLNE

ROCHDALE ○

Black Moss ●

OLDHAM ○

White Moss ●

▲ Black Hill 1908'

CROWDEN ●

MANCHESTER ○

Crowden ●

△ Bleaklow Hill 2061'

GLOSSOP ○

Kinder Scout 2088' △

● Edale

Grindsbrook ●

EDALE ●

▲ Castleton

R. MERSEY

STOCKPORT ○

── THE PENNINE WAY

▲ YOUTH HOSTELS

0 to 500 feet

500 to 1,000 feet

Over 1,000 feet

10
MILES

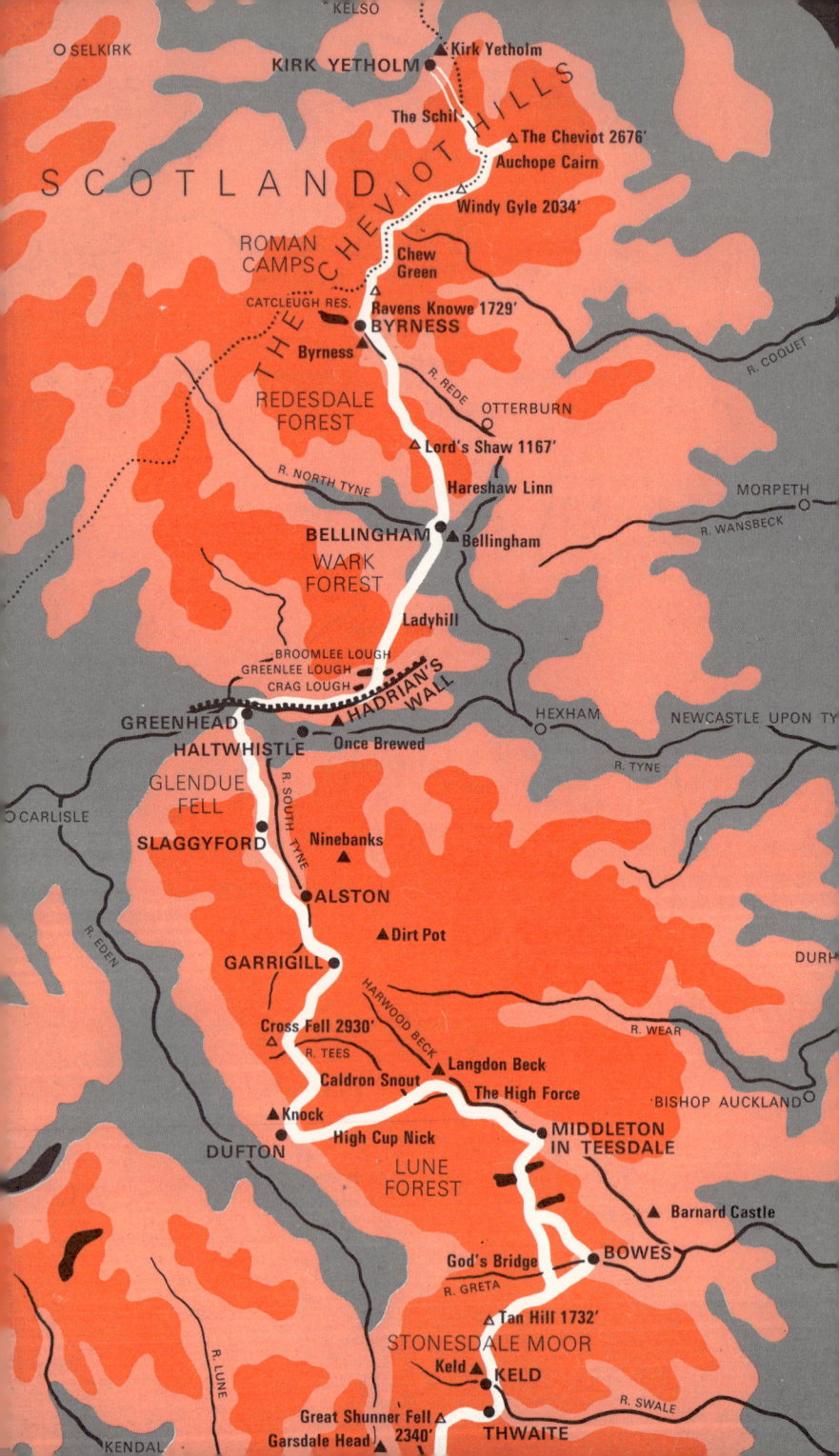